Japanese Americans and Internment

Consultant

Harry H.L. Kitano, PhD.

GLOBE FEARON
EDUCATIONAL PUBLISHER
PARAMUS, NEW JERSEY

Paramount

Paramount Publishing

Consultant:
Harry H. L. Kitano
Professor of Sociology
University of California at Los Angeles
Former Internee and co-author:
Japanese Americans: From Relocation to Redress

Executive Editor: Stephen Lewin
Editorial Consultant: Norman Lunger
Project Editor: Francie Holder
Editor: Bob Rahtz
Art Director: Nancy Sharkey
Production Manager: Penny Gibson
Project Manager: Walt Niedner
Senior Product Manager: Elmer Ildefonso
Book Design: Keithley & Associates
Electronic Page Production: Function Thru Form Inc.
Photo Research: Jenifer Hixson

Photo Acknowledgments:7: National Archives # 90-G-152-2038. 10, 13: UPI/Bettmann. 15: Bishop Museum. 21: UPI/Bettmann. 23: National Archives # 80-G-16871. 25: National Archives # 220-WR-176. 29: National Archives # 210-GA-36. 31, 33: UPI/Bettmann. 39: National Archives # 210-GA-35. 41: UPI/Bettmann. 43: National Archives # 210-GC-324. 53, 57: UPI/Bettmann Newsphotos. 61: National Archives # 210-GB-388. 67 69,71, 72: UPI/Bettmann. 81: Bettmann Archive. 83: Courtesy of the Gerald R. Ford Library. 85: AP/Wide World Photos.Cover: The Bettmann Archive

Cover: Los Angeles, 1942. Her world in turmoil, a Japanese American child waits for the bus that will take her and her family to an internment camp

Cover Design: Armando Baez

ISBN: 835 90623-X

Printed in the United States of America   2 3 4 5 6 7 8 9 10 98 97 96 94

GLOBE FEARON
EDUCATIONAL PUBLISHER
PARAMUS, NEW JERSEY

Paramount Publishing

CONTENTS

JAPANESE AMERICANS BEFORE WORLD WAR II, 1868–1940

THINKING ABOUT THE CHAPTER

What role did people of Japanese ancestry play in the United States in the years leading up to World War II?

SECTIONS

1 East to the Americas

2 A Closed Door

3 Making a New Life

Thankful that the long sea voyage from Japan was finally ending, Benko Nagashima (beng-koh nah-gah-shee-mah) was excited as the ship eased into the dock in Seattle. Wearing her best **kimono** (a wide-sleeved Japanese robe), she stared wide-eyed at the crowd of Japanese men who packed the landing below. The men were eagerly searching among the ship's passengers for the women who had sailed from Japan to be their brides.

The year was 1914. Many ships were carrying Japanese immigrants to the West Coast of the United States. Earlier, in the 1890s and early 1900s, almost all Japanese immigrants had been young men. They found jobs, worked hard, and sometimes returned to Japan to choose a wife. Others asked friends

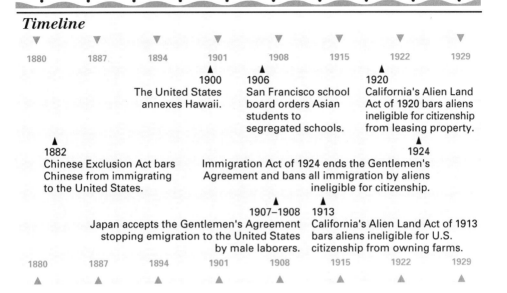

back home to help find suitable young women for them to marry. Since most Japanese marriages at that time were arranged by the parents of the bride and groom, marriages between strangers were not unusual. Many women traveled to the United States to marry men they had never seen. They were called **picture brides** because their husbands-to-be knew them only from photographs.

Unlike many of the women on the ship, however, Benko was not a picture bride. She was coming with her parents, two sisters, and two younger brothers to settle in the United States. Once settled, her parents arranged a marriage for Benko.

The story of Benko and her children, who were born in the United States, is typical of the stories of thousands of Japanese Americans from the 1860s through 1940. It is a story of the trials they faced and the triumphs they achieved. That is the subject of this chapter. However, when war broke out between Japan and the United States in 1941, a new period of heartbreak and pain opened. That period and its consequences are the subject of the rest of this book.

1 EAST TO THE AMERICAS

Why were thousands of Japanese drawn to the shores of the Americas during the late 19th and early 20th centuries?

For hundreds of years, Japan was closed to foreigners and isolated from the rest of the world. Few Japanese people had ever left the islands that made up their country. Although most of the people were poor, they were proud of their country and its traditions. Until the middle of the 19th century, most Japanese would not have considered finding a home in another part of the world.

New Era for Japan After 1868, major changes in Japanese life opened the way for the flow of Japanese settlers to other lands. For more than two centuries, Japan's rulers had not permitted Japanese subjects to travel to foreign countries. At the same time, the rulers had also kept foreigners out of Japan.

But Japan's policy of isolating itself from the outside world had an unexpected effect. As Western nations rushed ahead in technology and military power, Japan was left behind. All that began to change in 1853. In that year, a U.S. fleet led by Commodore Matthew C. Perry steamed into Tokyo Bay. Perry demanded that Japan open its ports to trade with the United States. Japanese leaders felt their nation was too weak to offer much resistance, so they yielded to Perry's demand.

The Japanese felt alarm and shame. Perry's action made it clear how far behind in technology Japan was. After a struggle for control, a new group of rulers took over the government, and a new era in Japan's history began. Under the Emperor Meiji (may-jee), who assumed the throne in 1868, Japan began a drive to modernize itself.

The modernization campaign greatly disrupted Japanese society. A new military draft forced all young men to serve in the army. To pay for modernization, the government placed new taxes on land. Both these policies placed a great burden on Japanese farm families, who made up the greater part of the Japanese population. Rumblings of dissatisfaction began to be heard in the countryside.

Japanese immigrants, including picture brides arrive at Angel island, California in 1911.

Contract Labor in Hawaii

About this time, sugar growers in Hawaii needed laborers for their plantations. The Japanese government saw a way to reduce unrest in the countryside by allowing workers to take jobs in Hawaii. Japanese in rural areas saw a chance to avoid the draft and perhaps increase their earnings. Between 1885 and 1900, tens of thousands of Japanese men and women went to Hawaii as **contract laborers**. Under this arrangement, a worker agreed to work for a certain period of time. At the time, Hawaii was an independent kingdom. However, most of its sugar plantations were owned by U.S. citizens.

Life on the plantations was very hard. The laborers were treated as little more than slaves. If they tried to escape before their contract was over, they would be captured and whipped.

In 1898, the United States **annexed,** or took control of Hawaii. Of the 154,000 people who lived there at the time, some 60,000 were of Japanese origin. Some of the Japanese residents of Hawaii then moved to the West Coast of the United States.

THE FIRST JAPANESE AMERICAN

Today, thousands of Japanese citizens pass through U.S. ports and airports every month. But when 13-year-old Hikozo Hamada (hee-koh-zoh hahm-ah-dah) landed in San Francisco in 1850, people stopped and stared. Few San Franciscans had ever seen a Japanese boy before.

Hikozo, in fact, had never expected to come to the United States. His journey began on a small Japanese ship that was sailing along the coast of Japan. A severe storm struck the ship. It snapped the mast and blew off the sail. For 50 days, Hikozo and his shipmates drifted at sea. Then a U.S. ship rescued them and brought them to San Francisco. After a year in port, the Japanese were able to start back to Japan. But Hikozo decided that he wanted to live in the United States.

Fortunately for Hikozo, an official in San Francisco named B.C. Sanders took an interest in him. He took the boy to the East Coast. In Baltimore, Hikozo learned English and joined the Roman Catholic Church. At his baptism, he took a new, more American-sounding name: Joseph Heco. Heco eventually was the first Japanese to become a U.S. citizen.

In the years to come, Joseph Heco had many interesting experiences. In Washington, D.C., he met President Abraham Lincoln in the White House. He served as an interpreter for U.S. diplomats in their dealings with Japanese officials. Joseph Heco spent the final years of his life in Japan, promoting good relations between the land of his birth and his adopted country.

Chinese and Japanese in the West The first immigrants from Asia to the U.S. West Coast came from China. Many white U.S. citizens objected to the presence of the Chinese. They feared that since the Chinese were willing to work for low wages, the Chinese would take jobs away from U.S. citizens. But anti-Chinese feeling was also due to **prejudice** (suspicion and hatred for people of different backgrounds). Responding to pressure from Californians and others, Congress in 1882 passed the **Chinese Exclusion Act**. This law banned all immigration to the United States by Chinese.

Before long, such anti-Chinese legislation would be applied to the Japanese who began to come to the United States. Japanese immigrants usually came from rural areas in Japan. Many times they were the oldest sons who had inherited family farms that were burdened with high taxes. Most of them intended to stay just long enough to earn money to pay the taxes or to build a home back in Japan. As one Japanese immigrant, Riichi Satow (rihch-ee sah-toh), explained:

> America was the first choice of places to go for almost everybody in Japan at that time. We thought lots of jobs were available and the wages were double because the dollar was worth twice as much as a yen [the Japanese unit of currency]. Our minds were filled with such dreams.

For some that dream came true. But for them and the many others for whom it did not come true, life in the United States was not easy.

TAKING ANOTHER LOOK

1. How did changes in Japanese society contribute to the flow of Japanese immigrants to the United States?
2. Why were Japanese people willing to go to Hawaii as contract laborers?
3. *CRITICAL THINKING* Imagine you are the oldest son of a Japanese farm family in 1900. What reasons would you give family members for wanting to emigrate to the United States?

2 A CLOSED DOOR

How did the United States discourage Japanese immigrants from coming to this country?

In the 1890s, people like Riichi Satow were welcomed by U.S. employers who saw the Japanese as a source of cheap labor. But the immigrants faced open hostility from many native-born Americans and European immigrants.

The Issei, the Nisei, and Others The Japanese who moved to the United States to start new lives referred to themselves as **Issei** (EE-say), which means first generation. Almost all of those who came before 1912 remained citizens of Japan. U.S. laws at the time allowed only "free white" persons or "persons of African nativity or descent" to become **naturalized** citizens, aliens granted citizenship.

However, according to the U.S. Constitution, U.S.-born children of Japanese immigrants held U.S. citizenship because they were born here. Children of Issei were called **Nisei** (nee-say), which means second generation. As time passed, the Nisei grew more and more numerous. Eventually they had children of their own. Children of Nisei were called **Sansei** (sahn-say), which means third generation.

Many Nisei shared the Japanese customs of their parents while at the same time adopting U.S. ways of thinking and acting. At home, they talked to their parents in Japanese, bowed respectfully to their elders, and ate foods like rice cakes and sweetened bean soup. At school, they spoke English, ate sandwiches, played baseball, and recited the "Pledge of Allegiance" like other U.S. citizens.

Hostility to Japanese and Japanese Americans is reflected in this sign telling them not to apply for farm work.

Facing Hostility From the beginning, cultural differences such as language, religion, and other ways of living set the Issei and Nisei apart from their neighbors. Prejudice was also an important factor. One of the first memories of a Japanese immigrant who landed in San Francisco in 1905 was of gangs of rowdy boys throwing horse dung at him.

A major international dispute over the Japanese in the United States arose in 1906. In that year, the San Francisco school board ordered all of the city's 93 Asian pupils to attend a separate, segregated school. The Japanese government regarded this action as an insult to Asians and protested sharply. President Theodore Roosevelt denounced the school board's action. But, in California, the President's statement merely strengthened anti-Japanese passions. One San Francisco newspaper accused Roosevelt of being unpatriotic. The paper claimed that the President was uniting "with aliens [non-citizens] to break down the civilization of his own countrymen."

Gentlemen's Agreement After long discussions, Roosevelt arranged a settlement. The school board agreed that the Asian children, both Japanese and Chinese, could continue to attend schools with other students. During 1907-1908, U.S. and Japanese diplomats also reached a series of understandings that became known as the **Gentlemen's Agreement**. Japan said it would no longer let laborers and artisans go to the United States. Henceforth, only businesspeople, students, picture brides, and family members of U.S. residents would be allowed to go. Japanese immigration was reduced to a mere trickle.

More Restrictions The Gentlemen's Agreement did not end anti-Japanese feeling. Hostility to the Japanese continued to grow in the years after 1908. Many states passed new laws that restricted the rights of the Japanese. California's **Alien Land Law of 1913** set a pattern followed by several other Western states. The law forbade the purchase of farm land by "aliens ineligible to citizenship." Because Asians could not become citizens, Japanese, Chinese, Korean, and other Asian aliens were unable to buy farms.

For Issei like Riichi Satow, the new law meant that by the time he had saved enough money to buy land for a strawberry farm, he had no right to own a farm at all. But

Satow, like many others, found a way around the law. He bought land in the names of his U.S.-born children. Since the Nisei children were U.S. citizens, the Alien Land Law did not apply to them. In this way, many children who were not yet old enough to go to school became landowners.

In 1920, California passed a second Alien Land Law to close loopholes in the 1913 law. It barred Japanese citizens from leasing land. But again some Japanese got around such restrictions. They formed companies headed by white friends. The corporations bought land and redistributed to Japanese farmers to operate.

Shutting Out All Asian Immigrants Anti-Japanese forces scored their greatest triumph in 1924. In that year, Congress passed the **Immigration Act of 1924**, which ended immigration for all "aliens ineligible to citizenship." This meant that since Japanese and other Asians could not become citizens, they would no longer be admitted to the United States.

Suddenly, Japanese families in the United States found themselves cut off from their roots in Japan. One man had left his Japanese-born son to be raised by the boy's grandparents in Japan. Now, the son, who was past the age of 18, could not join his father in the United States. Other Japanese immigrants had planned to bring aging parents over from Japan after establishing a home here. The new law made that impossible.

TAKING ANOTHER LOOK

1. What was the effect of the Immigration Act of 1924?
2. *CRITICAL THINKING* What problems might develop for the Nisei because they shared two cultures?

3 MAKING A NEW LIFE

How did people of Japanese ancestry adapt to life in the United States?

Hanayo Inouye (hah-neye-oh ih-noh-way) was a picture bride (see page 4) with rosy dreams of life in a new land. When she arrived in San Francisco, her new husband

Long hours, hard work, and a slow rise to a better life were typical of Japanese farmworkers in California.

told her, "We are going to the country. You'd better not put good clothes on." She soon discovered why. Their first home was a corner of a barn on a large farm owned by a white citizen. They shared the barn with horses.

The next day, Hanayo began her new life, working on a crew that pruned grape vines in a vineyard. Her husband worked beside her. They toiled ten hours a day, for which they were paid three dollars. "When all the work was over for the season," she later recalled, "we went to a boarding house called the Hiroshima-ya, and waited for the next job." After many years of such work, Hanayo and her husband took better and better jobs until they were given the responsibility of managing a ranch.

The Inouyes' experience was typical—long hours, hard work, and a slow rise to a better life. Japanese "pioneers" like them did their work and put money aside from their poor earnings for the future.

Potato King Like other immigrant groups, the Japanese had their rags-to-riches stories. One of them was the story of George Shima, the potato king of the San Joaquin [SAN wah-KEEN] Valley. Shima came to the United States in 1889 at the age of 24. He worked first as a servant in a white family's home, then as a farm laborer and **labor contractor**, a person who supplies crews to farmers. Seeking further challenges, he made a deal with a California fruit

13

farmer, who let him grow onions and potatoes between rows of fruit trees.

Shima used the money earned from those crops and from his other work to lease land and buy property. This was in the years before the California laws that prevented Japanese from buying farm land. One of Shima's purchases was a group of swampy islands at the mouth of the San Joaquin River near Stockton, California. Shima put up dikes and dug ditches to drain the lands so that he could plant potatoes there. By the time he was in his 40s, he was supplying potatoes to a wide market and had become known as the potato king. Shima became a millionaire, owning fleets of barges, tugboats, and steamboats to carry his potatoes from Stockton to San Francisco.

Many Occupations Like Shima, a majority of the Japanese immigrants settled in California and worked in agriculture. Japanese communities also sprang up in Oregon, Washington, and other states. Other farmers marveled at the way the Japanese could coax a crop from small strips of land that no one else wanted to farm.

Some people of Japanese ancestry worked in areas other than agriculture. Some Japanese men worked for railroads, repairing and laying tracks. Others labored in coal and copper mines in Colorado, Wyoming, and other Western states. In many cities, Japanese families operated shops that sold fruits, vegetables, and fish.

Different Faiths Most of the Japanese who came to the United States were followers of the Buddhist faith. Buddhism was and is one of the main religions of Japan. Christians made up another major group among the Japanese immigrants.

Life in the Japanese communities of the United States often centered around the Buddhist temple or Christian church. There, priests or pastors conducted services in the Japanese language. Some temples and churches sponsored English classes.

Trying to Fit In Both the Issei and the Nisei kept alive old traditions that were important parts of Japanese culture. One such tradition was to honor the Japanese emperor on

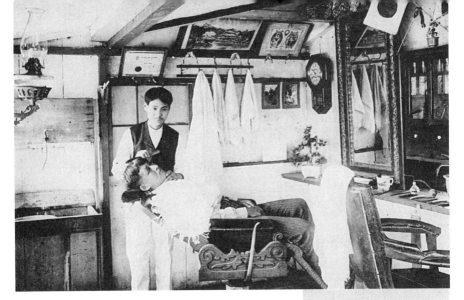

Inside a barbershop run by a Japanese American in Hawaii old traditions were preserved.

his birthday with elaborate ceremonies. But this and similar activities served to fuel suspicions that U.S. citizens often had of their Japanese American neighbors. To whom did the Japanese Americans feel their greatest loyalty? To the emperor or to the United States?

One Nisei who was in her teens during the 1930s had no doubts. "Neither my sister nor I, as children, ever considered ourselves anything other than Americans," she later wrote. "At school we saluted the American flag and learned to become good citizens."

Yet, like other Japanese Americans, she felt the sting of rejection. In high school and college, her classmates never invited her to their social functions such as school dances. If she wanted to go to a restaurant or hairdresser, she called first to ask if they accepted Japanese clients. Many did not.

During the 1930s, war clouds were gathering. Japan and the United States stood on opposite sides of the coming world struggle. For people of Japanese ancestry in the United States, new trials were about to begin.

TAKING ANOTHER LOOK

1. How did most Japanese immigrants make a living in the United States?

2. *CRITICAL THINKING* How did maintaining some old Japanese traditions help Japanese immigrants in the United States? How did they work to their disadvantage?

CHAPTER 1: CLOSE UP

1 East to the Americas

- The drive to modernize Japan in the late 19th century forced many Japanese to emigrate to other countries.
- Hawaii served as a steppingstone for many Japanese who eventually went to the U.S. mainland.

2 A Closed Door

- Japanese immigrants were barred from U.S. citizenship, but their U.S.-born children were automatically citizens.
- Western states placed legal restrictions on the rights of Japanese and other immigrants from Asia.
- The Immigration Act of 1924 shut off immigration from Japan and the rest of Asia.

3 Making a New Life

- Japanese immigrants to the United States worked mainly in agriculture, although some took jobs in fishing, mining, and other industries.
- Most Japanese immigrants were Buddhists, although there were also some Christians.
- Americans of Japanese ancestry faced many forms of discrimination and rejection in their everyday lives.

WHO, WHAT, WHERE

1. **What** traditional clothing did Japanese women sometimes wear?
2. **What** does it mean to be naturalized?
3. **Where** did many Japanese go to become contract laborers between 1885 and 1900?
4. **What** changes in Japan brought about the migration in the late 1800s from the country?
5. **Who** were the first Japanese who emigrated from Japan?
6. **What** kinds of people were most likely to be hostile to Japanese immigrants? Why?
7. **Who** were the Issei, the Nisei, and the Sansei?

1. How did the goals of many Japanese immigrants change after they had settled in the United States?

2. How did Japanese immigrants differ from their non-Japanese neighbors in the United States?

3. How did the outlook and habits of the Nisei differ from those of the Issei?

4. Why were many Americans suspicious of or hostile to people of Japanese ancestry?

MAKING CONNECTIONS

1. What was the connection between the arrival in Tokyo Bay of Commodore Perry's ships and Japan's program of rapid modernization?

2. What was the connection between the Gentlemen's Agreement and declining Japanese immigration to the United States?

WRITING ABOUT HISTORY

1. Imagine that you are a picture bride or picture groom. Write a letter to a close friend describing your feelings as you are about to meet your new spouse.

2. Describe the life of a recently arrived Japanese immigrant on the West Coast early in the 20th century.

3. Imagine that you are a young Japanese immigrant to the United States. You left your parents in Japan, expecting to save money and return, but you have decided to stay in this country. Compose a letter to your family in Japan explaining your decision.

4. Imagine that you are a Nisei in the 1930s. Write a letter to a newspaper protesting against discrimination you have experienced.

CHAPTER 2

PEARL HAR- BOR AND THE DECISION TO INTERN

How did U.S. involvement in World War II affect people of Japanese descent living in the United States?

December 7, 1941, dawned sunny and bright in Honolulu. A high-school honor student, 17-year-old Japanese American Dan Inouye (ih-noh-way), heard the shocking news on the radio as he prepared for Sunday breakfast. "This is not a test! Pearl Harbor is being bombed by the Japanese!" Alarmed and frightened, Dan and his Japanese-born father saw smoke rising from the naval base nearby. He later recalled:

> And then we saw the planes. They came zooming up out of that sea of gray smoke, flying north toward where we stood, . . . and if it hadn't been for that red ball on their wings, the rising sun of

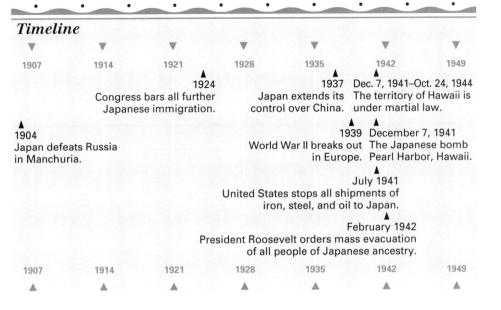

1907   1914   1921   1928   1935   1942   1949

1924
Congress bars all further
Japanese immigration.

1904
Japan defeats Russia
in Manchuria.

1937   Dec. 7, 1941–Oct. 24, 1944
Japan extends its   The territory of Hawaii is
control over China.   under martial law.

1939   December 7, 1941
World War II breaks out   The Japanese bomb
in Europe.   Pearl Harbor, Hawaii.

July 1941
United States stops all shipments of
iron, steel, and oil to Japan.

February 1942
President Roosevelt orders mass evacuation
of all people of Japanese ancestry.

1907   1914   1921   1928   1935   1942   1949

the Japanese Empire, you could easily believe that they were Americans, flying over in precise military salute.

The attack killed more than 2,400 people and plunged the United States into a bitter war against Japan. In the days after Pearl Harbor, Dan Inouye went to classes as usual. Night after night, he worked at a first-aid station, helping to care for war victims. Yet on the streets, Dan faced abuse from people who thought that anyone who looked Japanese was an enemy. Throughout the United States, many Japanese Americans had similar experiences.

Japanese Americans like Dan Inouye, who later became a U.S. senator from Hawaii, feared they would be branded traitors. No matter how hard they worked in war relief efforts, no matter how carefully they obeyed war regulations, no matter how many war bonds they bought, they could not avoid suspicious eyes and hostile comments. Not while the war raged on.

1 PRELUDE TO WAR

What was the background of Japan's attack on the United States?

A few days before the raid on Pearl Harbor, U.S. intelligence agents intercepted a startling message. The message had been sent by the Japanese government in Tokyo to the Japanese embassy in Washington, D.C. Burn secret codes, the message said.

A U.S. Army officer was sent to the embassy on Massachusetts Avenue. Looking over the back fence, he saw embassy employees burning papers. Did this mean that the Japanese were preparing for war? U.S. officials thought so. But they expected Japan to attack targets in Asia, not in Hawaii.

The Japanese attack followed years of rising tension between Japan and the United States. The immediate cause of the tension was a war between Japan and the U.S.-backed government of China. But its roots could be traced back much further, to the Meiji modernization of Japan in the 19th century (see page 6). The modernization policies had turned Japan from an isolated island nation into a military world power.

Japan Steps Onto the World Stage The islands that make up Japan have few of the natural resources needed by a modern nation. To get iron ore and petroleum to run its industries, Japan's leaders had to look abroad. Japan had little to offer in trade, other than silks and other textiles. Therefore, Japan decided to imitate the European powers. It turned to **imperialism**—the conquest of foreign lands.

The military power that Japan developed in less than 30 years surprised other nations. In 1895, Japan won a brief war against China. In the years that followed, Japan and Russia jockeyed for control of the many resources in the Chinese province of Manchuria.

Japanese-Russian competition reached a crisis in 1904. Negotiations were held between Russia and Japan. However, the two countries could not agree on the areas of

After a phony "incident" Japanese soldiers invaded Manchuria in 1931. They defeated the Chinese army and took over much of the area.

Manchuria each nation would control. Japan's navy attacked the Russian fleet anchored at Port Arthur in Manchuria, and the Russo-Japanese War began. At sea and on land, Japan overpowered the Russians. In 1905, at U.S. President Roosevelt's invitation, the Japanese and Russians signed a peace treaty at Portsmouth, New Hampshire. The terms of the agreement made Japan the clear victor.

Falling Out U.S. sympathies in the war had been with Japan. Japan appeared to be the underdog in the dispute with aggressive Russia, a huge country that stretched across two continents and was ruled by a **czar** (king). Japan seemed to return the friendly feelings of the United States. In 1909, President Roosevelt sent the U.S. Navy on a round-the-world tour. On a stop in Japan, the fleet was warmly welcomed. Thousands of Japanese children turned out to sing "The Star-Spangled Banner."

However, such friendly moments between the United States and Japan became fewer and fewer in the years that followed. Each nation found fault with the other. People in the United States were shocked when Japan made Korea its colony in 1910. Japan protested when California passed its discriminatory land law in 1913 (see page 11). In 1924, when Congress barred all further Japanese immigration (see page 12), violent anti-U.S. protests rocked Japan.

Effects of the World Depression In the 1930s, what came to be known as the Great Depression spread throughout the world. Living standards dropped. One nation after another tried to protect its own businesses by raising trade barriers. The Japanese, who relied on trade with other nations, grew more and more alarmed. If other nations would not buy Japan's products, the nation would have no money to pay for its essential imports. How would its industries run if they could not get raw materials? How would its army and navy operate?

As the misery of the Great Depression grew, so did violent unrest in Japanese politics. Assassins killed government officials whose policies they did not like. Nationalists called for expansion abroad. They eyed the rich farmlands and coal and iron mines of Manchuria. Although both Russia and Japan had important financial stakes in Manchuria, the region was still officially a part of China.

War in Manchuria and China In 1931, an explosion damaged a Japanese-controlled railroad in Manchuria. It was later revealed that a group of Japanese army officers had staged the incident to provide an excuse to invade Manchuria. The Japanese army attacked the Chinese troops there and soon took over much of the region. When the **League of Nations** (an association of nations organized to promote international peace and cooperation) condemned Japan for its army's actions, Japan withdrew from the League.

In 1937, Japan extended its control in a full-scale war with China. Within a year, it controlled most of eastern China. Japanese leaders now spoke of establishing a great empire, which they called the "Greater East Asia Co-Prosperity Sphere."

The United States Applies Pressure Responding to Japan's assault on China, U.S. President Franklin D. Roosevelt condemned Japan as an aggressor and sent U.S. aid

Japanese surprise attack on Pearl Harbor brought the United States into World War II.

to China. Roosevelt also applied economic pressure. He placed an **embargo**, or ban, on military goods for Japan. Many Americans also began to **boycott**, or refuse to purchase, Japanese goods.

Japan's military could not do without the vital supplies the United States had been providing. In 1940, the military leaders therefore launched a war for control of resource-rich lands in a wide band from Thailand to the Dutch East Indies (now Indonesia). In July 1941, the United States responded by stopping all shipments of scrap iron, steel, and oil to Japan. The Japanese attack on Pearl Harbor in December of that year was aimed at crippling the U.S. Navy so that it could not interfere with Japan's sweep into southeastern Asia.

The United States Prepares for War Japan's attack on Pearl Harbor came more than two years after World War II had started in Europe. From 1939 to 1941, the United States had managed to stay out of the European war. However, when Nazi Germany defeated France and occupied much of Western Europe in 1940, Congress decided to build up the U.S. armed forces. It passed the first peacetime draft in U.S. history. Among the 16 million men who registered for the draft were 42,000 Japanese Americans. At the time of Pearl Harbor, 1,500 Japanese Americans were serving with the army in Hawaii. The navy, however, did not accept Japanese Americans.

TAKING ANOTHER LOOK

1. In what way did Japan's lack of natural resources influence its foreign policy?
2. How did the worldwide Great Depression threaten Japan?
3. *CRITICAL THINKING* What impact do you think Japan's aggression in China and southeastern Asia had on the lives of Japanese Americans?

2 MASS EVACUATION

Why did U.S. officials decide in February 1942 to round up all people of Japanese ancestry living near the West Coast?

Sudden knocks on the door. Arrests in the night. Prison camps for "dangerous" people. Those were things that most U.S. citizens associated with police states like Nazi Germany. But these events happened in the United States in the days that followed Pearl Harbor.

At first, the arrests were limited. They targeted people living in the United States who were **enemy aliens**, or citizens of enemy nations, who were on a list of "dangerous persons." That meant mainly Japanese, Germans, and Italians. Germany and Italy were allies of Japan. They declared war on the United States four days after Pearl Harbor.

But in February 1942, President Roosevelt took a drastic step that went beyond dealing with enemy aliens. He ordered the mass evacuation of all people of Japanese ancestry who were living on the West Coast. That included U.S. citizens as well as Japanese citizens. The army rounded up more than 120,000 people. It sent them to ten isolated internment camps that the government deceptively called "relocation centers". For the first time in U.S. history, the U.S. government took away freedom from people of a par-

NOTICE

Headquarters
~ern Defense Command
and Fourth Army

Exclusion Order No. 1

Western Defense Command and Fourth Army
Wartime Civil Control Administration

INSTRUCTIONS TO ALL
JAPANESE
Living on Bainbridge Island

In the days after Pearl Harbor, U.S. authorities arrested many Japanese and expelled many Japanese Americans from their homes.

ticular ancestry. Japanese and Japanese Americans were placed behind barbed wire, guarded by soldiers. This was done although the government had not accused them of any wrongdoing or of breaking any law.

Why did the government decide on this move? How could it imprison U.S. citizens without even accusing them of crimes? Why were only people of Japanese ancestry rounded up, and not the millions of people of German or Italian ancestry? Those are serious questions that Americans are still asking themselves more than 50 years after the evacuation took place. To supply even partial answers to these questions, we must understand the state of mind of the country in the days and weeks following the attack on Pearl Harbor.

First Steps: Arrests of Enemy Aliens After the shock of the Pearl Harbor attack, the U.S. government moved quickly to prevent actions that would weaken the country's ability to fight the war. Dwight Takashi Uchida (tah-kah-shee oo-chee-dah) was an executive in the San Francisco offices of Mitsui and Company, a giant Japanese firm. Soon after Pearl Harbor, he felt the hand of the government. Uchida was on a list of possible enemy agents. Within hours of the attack, FBI agents rapped on the door of his home. No one answered the agents' knock. They knocked again. Then they broke in and searched the house. When Uchida returned home, they arrested him.

Uchida was among the 1,300 Japanese citizens who were rounded up by U.S. authorities in the hours and days after Pearl Harbor. Many German and Italian citizens were also arrested. Some were released. Others, like Uchida, were **interned**, or confined in prison camps.

Many of the Japanese arrested were community leaders—business executives, scholars, priests, and pastors. Others were operators of fishing boats whose work might allow them to spy on military ship movements.

Looking for Illegal Possessions U.S. authorities feared a Japanese invasion. They declared the West Coast and Alaska a military "theater of operations." Throughout the country, Japanese aliens were forbidden to possess guns, explosives, shortwave radios, and even cameras. Raiding teams searched aliens' homes, looking for such illegal possessions.

The raids frightened the Japanese community. People looked through their homes to find items that might arouse suspicion. One boy threw out a toy Japanese sword. A woman burned her prize collection of Japanese literature.

Those who did not destroy suspicious items later wished they had. Masuo Yasui (mah-soo-oh yah-soo-ee), who operated an orchard in Oregon, was accused of being a spy when a search of his home turned up drawings of the Panama Canal. Yasui insisted they were part of a school assignment by one of his young sons. At a hearing, a prosecutor expressed disbelief. "Didn't you have these maps and diagrams of the canal so you could direct the blowing up of the locks?" the prosecutor asked. "Prove that you didn't plan to blow up the Panama Canal!" Yasui was held in internment camps until five months after Japan surrendered.

ELSEWHERE IN THE HEMISPHERE

Many countries in the Western Hemisphere other than the United States also included people of Japanese descent among their populations. They varied in their treatment of these people during World War II.

Canada carried out its own mass evacuation of citizens and aliens. Almost all of Canada's 22,000 residents of Japanese ancestry lived in British Columbia, on the Pacific coast directly north of Washington state. Three fourths of them held Canadian citizenship. Beginning in February 1942, Japanese Canadians were placed in special camps away from the coast. At the end of the war, the Canadian government ordered the deportation to Japan of thousands of Japanese Canadians and Japanese aliens. This was not just a result of wartime prejudices but a part of a campaign begun 50 years earlier to make British Columbia a province of British white people only. It was not until 1949 that deported Japanese Canadians could return to homes along Canada's Pacific coast.

Brazil, which faced east onto the Atlantic, left its 250,000 Japanese residents alone. However, Mexico, with 10,000 Japanese, created a 62-mile zone around its coasts and borders. All Japanese were removed from this area by the end of March 1942.

A half century later, people of Japanese ancestry had won acceptance in Peru. In 1990, the people of Peru elected Alberto Fujimori (foo-jee-mohr-ee) to be their president. It was a sweet moment for the South American nation's 55,000 people of Japanese descent. At the start of World War II, Peru had shown little regard for its Japanese residents. It sent 1,800 Japanese aliens to detention camps in Texas. It also confiscated businesses that belonged to Japanese residents. After the war, the Japanese Peruvians were threatened with deportation to Japan since they had entered the United States without proper visas and Peru refused to readmit them.

Public Hostility It was not only officials who held such anti-Japanese views. Americans were bitter over the Pearl Harbor attack. Public worry over Japanese victories in the Pacific increased anti-Japanese feelings. These were strengthened when the U.S. secretary of the navy asserted that Japanese American "traitors" in Hawaii had helped to prepare the surprise attack on Pearl Harbor. (Official studies later found no evidence to support the charge.)

Certain columnists and radio commentators helped to whip up hysteria against people of Japanese ancestry. Henry McLemore, a newspaper columnist, wrote:

> I am for immediate removal of every Japanese on the West Coast to a point deep in the interior. Herd 'em up, pack 'em off and give 'em the inside room in the badlands. Let 'em be pinched, hurt, hungry. . . . Personally, I hate the Japanese. And that goes for all of them.

Racism was certainly one element of the anti-Japanese feeling. However, economic rivalry and greed also played a part. Farmers and business people saw a chance to eliminate Japanese competitors. Evacuation would allow many people to "make a buck"—often, "lots of bucks." (You will read more about about this in Chapter 3.)

Debating Evacuation Within the U.S. government, officials debated what to do. Many military leaders argued that Japanese Americans should be removed from the West Coast. They said people of Japanese descent might blow up crucial facilities like the Boeing aircraft factories around Seattle, or that they might spy on military bases.

Demands for evacuation were widespread. Public-opinion polls showed that two thirds of the public wanted the United States to concentrate on fighting Japan rather than Nazi Germany. However, President Roosevelt believed it was essential to focus first on the war in Europe. Moreover, Roosevelt was reluctant to go against the advice of his military leaders who wanted the war effort centered in Europe first. Getting tough with Japanese Americans would be a signal to the public that the President did not take the Pacific war lightly, yet it would allow him to emphasize the European struggle.

February 1942: Evacuation Order By February 19, ten weeks after Pearl Harbor, Roosevelt had made up his mind. On that day he signed Executive Order 9066. The order authorized the secretary of war to name "military areas" from which "any or all persons" might be evacuated. Despite the order's wording, it was clearly aimed at Japanese Americans alone. Historian Roger Daniels has written: "It may well have been the most popular home-front action of the federal government during the entire war." However, a few lonely voices criticized Roosevelt's decision. Columnist Chester Rowell of the San Francisco Chronicle cautioned:

> The order applies, in principle, to all of us, including American Indians, or those whose ancestors came over on the *Mayflower*. The rights of

Executive Order 9066 banning Japanese Americans from "military areas" was well received by the press and by the American public.

any of us, to live in our own homes, to move about, or the conditions under which we may do so, are subject to the sole will of the commanding general.

But the nation was at war, people were fearful, and Rowell's warning was ignored.

TAKING ANOTHER LOOK

1. How did the February 1942 evacuation decision differ from actions taken in December 1941?
2. On what grounds did columnist Rowell criticize Order 9066?
3. *CRITICAL THINKING* Why do you think the government evacuated people of Japanese descent but not those of German or Italian ancestry?

3 THE DIFFERENCE IN HAWAII

How were people of Japanese ancestry in Hawaii treated during the war?

Almost before the bombs stopped falling on Pearl Harbor, rumors began to fly in Hawaii. One report said that local Japanese residents had poisoned Honolulu's water supply. Another claimed that some of the 45 airmen from Japan who were killed at Pearl Harbor had been wearing high-school rings from Honolulu's McKinley High School. Still another story told how someone had carefully slashed a giant arrow through a field of sugar cane to guide the attacking planes toward Pearl Harbor.

All the rumors were false. Despite claims of "traitorous" actions by local residents, only one hostile act was ever confirmed. A lone Japanese American on the island of Niihau gave assistance to a downed Japanese flier. Then he committed suicide. Hawaiians of Japanese descent proved as loyal as any other Americans during the war.

Martial Law On December 7, 1941, there were 157,00 people of Japanese ancestry living in Hawaii. In California, roughly 2 percent of the people were of Japanese ancestry. In Hawaii's multiethnic society, the percentage was far higher—37 percent. Four fifths of these people were U.S. citizens. In other words, about one Hawaiian in every three was of Japanese ancestry. Their numbers and importance in Hawaiian society made a difference in how they were treated.

At the start of the war, the federal government placed Hawaii under **martial law**. That meant that soldiers patrolled the streets and administered the laws. No state on the U.S. mainland took such drastic action.

Under martial law, many democratic freedoms were curbed. Everyone on the islands had to obey travel restrictions and submit to a **curfew** (a time after which people cannot leave their houses). For people of Japanese descent, the curfew was longer and the rules stricter than for other Hawaiians.

No General Roundup Within hours after the attack on Pearl Harbor, federal agents in Hawaii began picking up Japanese aliens who were on a "dangerous" list. The next day the government opened a detention center on Sand Island in Honolulu Harbor. Hundreds of Japanese were held there.

Unlike Japanese Americans on the West Coast of the United States, Japanese Americans in Hawaii were allowed to stay in their homes and go to their schools.

In mid-December 1941, President Roosevelt's advisers proposed moving all Japanese aliens in Hawaii onto Molokai, then known as the island for lepers (people with a disease that attacks the skin and nerves). But the move never took place. The U.S. military commander for Hawaii successfully resisted any full-scale roundup of enemy aliens. Publicly, he declared:

> We must remember that this is America and we must do things the American way. . . . We must not knowingly and deliberately deny any loyal citizen the opportunity of exercising or demonstrating his loyalty in a concrete way.

In reports to his superiors, he mentioned a further reason—Hawaii's economy depended on the work done by people of Japanese descent. Without them, the economy would collapse. Unlike the Japanese Americans on the West Coast, they were never subjected to mass evacuation.

Demonstrating Loyalty Japanese Americans living in Hawaii found many ways to demonstrate their loyalty. Dan Inouye, as you have read, helped tend the wounded (see page 18). Throughout the war, others donated blood or patrolled the beaches against the threat of invasion.

A number of Japanese Americans had joined military reserve units such as the Hawaii Territorial Guard. In January 1942, their commanders told them that they were being released from duty. Their services were "no longer needed." Eager to prove their patriotism, the young Nisei sent a petition to the Hawaiian military commander. It declared:

> . . . Hawaii is our home; the United States, our country. We know but one Loyalty and that is to the Stars and Stripes. We wish to do our part as loyal Americans in every way possible and we hereby offer ourselves for whatever service you may see fit to use us.

Eager to prove their patriotism, members of the Hawaii National Guard kept the unit from being disbanded. They provided valuable help to the U.S. Army Corps of Engineers.

Impressed, the commander allowed the young Nisei to form a special labor battalion to help the Corps of Engineers. The battalion cut rock from quarries, repaired bridges, built roads, and did other essential tasks. Its members were called Varsity Victory Volunteers, or **VVV**.

Later in the war, Japanese Americans would take a far more direct role in the nation's defense (see Chapter 5).

TAKING ANOTHER LOOK

1. What restrictions were placed on the freedom of people in Hawaii, especially those of Japanese ancestry?
2. How did Japanese Hawaiians show their loyalty?
3. *CRITICAL THINKING* Why do you think that most of the people of Japanese descent in Hawaii were not relocated and interned as people were on the mainland?

CHAPTER 2: CLOSE UP

1 Prelude to War

- The modernization policies that started under Emperor Meiji turned Japan into an industrial and military power.
- The need for raw materials helped spur Japanese attacks on Manchuria and China in the 1930s.
- The United States cut off supplies of oil and war materials in response to Japan's aggressions against China and southeastern Asia.
- Japan's attack on Pearl Harbor was designed to prevent the United States from interfering with Japan's drive to gain control over resource-rich lands in southeastern Asia.

2 Mass Evacuation

- Immediately after the attack on Pearl Harbor, U.S. authorities rounded up people on a list of "dangerous" enemy aliens.
- Ten weeks later, President Roosevelt approved a mass evacuation of all people of Japanese descent, citizens and aliens alike, from the West Coast.
- Among the reasons for the evacuation decision were prejudice, a hope for economic gain among competitors of Japanese Americans, a fear that Japanese Americans might sabotage the war effort, and President Roosevelt's desire to win support for his "Europe-first" war policies.

3 The Difference in Hawaii

- After Pearl Harbor, Hawaii was governed by the U.S. military under martial law.
- People of Japanese descent made up more than one third of Hawaii's population and played a very important part in its economy.
- Thus, no mass evacuation of Japanese Hawaiians took place.

WHO, WHAT, WHERE

1. **Where** is Manchuria and why was it important to Japan?
2. **What** countries were Japan's allies in World War II?
3. **Where** is Pearl Harbor?
4. **What** are enemy aliens?

5. **What** was Executive Order 9066?
6. **What** is martial law?
7. **What** is a curfew?
8. **Who** were the Varsity Victory Volunteers?

UNDERSTANDING THE CHAPTER

1. Why did Japan wish to establish an empire in Manchuria, China, and southeastern Asia?
2. How did the Great Depression promote extremism in Japanese politics?
3. How did President Franklin D. Roosevelt respond to Japan's military attack on China?
4. How did Roosevelt's decision to concentrate first on the war in Europe influence his actions toward Japanese Americans?
5. What factors led to the U.S. policy of evacuating Japanese Americans from the West Coast?
6. How did the U.S. government's treatment of Japanese Americans in Hawaii differ from its treatment of Japanese Americans living along the West Coast?

MAKING CONNECTIONS

1. What was the connection between the U.S. cutoff of vital supplies to Japan and the Japanese decision to attack Pearl Harbor?
2. What was the connection between anti-Japanese prejudice and the decision to evacuate Japanese Americans from the West Coast?

WRITING ABOUT HISTORY

1. Write a newspaper editorial that might have been published in the 1930's stating how the United States should respond to Japanese actions in China.
2. Imagine that you are a Japanese American shopkeeper in December 1941. Write a letter to post on your shop window telling of your reactions to the attack on Pearl Harbor.

THE UPROOTING

THINKING ABOUT THE CHAPTER

How did evacuation orders affect the people of Japanese ancestry who lived in the restricted zones?

SECTIONS

- 1 Saying Goodbye
- 2 First Stop: Assembly Center
- 3 Lonely Exile

As her family's evacuation day approached, Emi Somekawa (ehm-ee soh-may-kah-wah) became sadder and sadder. People of Japanese descent had been ordered to **evacuate**, or leave, the coastal region of the western United States. "Why us?" she wondered. From the window of her home in Portland, Oregon, the young nurse could look across at her neighbors. Like her, they traced their ancestry to an enemy nation. "They were as German as German could be," Somekawa said, "and they were free. Why us? I felt like we were just being punished for nothing." On the day of the evacuation, a German American neighbor brought over a cake as a gesture of friendship. Later, the German American neighbors visited the Somekawas in the camp.

Timeline

December 1941	February 1942	April 1942	June 1942	August 1942	October 1942	December 1942

March 2, 1942
Evacuation areas created along the U.S. West Coast.

May 21, 1942
First group of evacuees leaves Portland assembly center.

Aug. 7, 1942
Government announces that evacuation is completed.

Dec. 7, 1941
Japan attacks Pearl Harbor.

Oct. 1. 1942
Permission granted for evacuees to seek residence outside relocation centers if they meet certain conditions.

Feb. 19, 1942
Executive Order 9066 authorizes military areas from which "any or all persons" might be evacuated.

Nov. 3, 1942
Last evacuees reach relocation centers from assembly camps.

December 1941	February 1942	April 1942	June 1942	August 1942	October 1942	December 1942

It was a spring of sad leave-takings, that spring of 1942. Up and down the West Coast, Japanese American families were preparing to evacuate and leave the towns, cities, and farms where they lived. Soon they would board the buses and trains that would carry them away. The reluctant **evacuees**, the people to be evacuated, wondered if they would ever again see their homes and their non-Japanese friends.

1 SAYING GOODBYE

What special hardships did people face as they prepared for the forced evacuation?

The first signs of the coming evacuation were notices printed in newspapers or pasted on store windows in Japanese neighborhoods: "Going out of business sale." "Must sell." "For sale: car, refrigerator, furniture. Cheap."

The evacuees could take only two bags each. How could they squeeze the possessions of a lifetime into two bundles? They could not, of course. They would have to sell what they could not stuff into two bags. Because they had only a matter of days, or a few weeks at most, before evacuation, they would accept almost any price they could get.

Some greedy and envious people saw the forced evacuation as a great financial opportunity and therefore supported the government policy. They realized that the internment of people of Japanese ancestry gave them a chance to eliminate business competition. They took advantage of the evacuees' predicament and purchased farms, businesses, and other valuable assets for almost nothing.

Who Will Keep the Business Going? Among those evacuees with the greatest difficulties were the owners of businesses. Jenjuro Shibata (jehn-joo-roh shee-bah-tah) ran a plant nursery near San Francisco. After Pearl Harbor, he lost his crop of Christmas roses when the gas company cut off the fuel he needed to heat his greenhouses. The company claimed it could no longer do business with enemy aliens. When evacuation time came, Shibata still owed a debt to a lumber merchant and could not pay. But the merchant proved to be one of the few people at the time to be understanding. He said, "Mr. Shibata, when you come back, we will talk about it. Don't be away too long."

Some Japanese businesspeople were able to keep ownership of their businesses. They hired others to run them while they were away. However, the arrangements did not always work out. Keisaburo Koda (kay-sah-byoo-rah koh-dah), a large rice grower in the San Joaquin Valley, discovered after the war that his rice mill and two thirds of his land had been sold without his knowledge. He received nothing from the sale.

What About My Education? At colleges and universities along the West Coast, Japanese American students rushed to finish their exams. But seniors missed the pomp and ceremony of graduation. Young Yoshiko Uchida (yoh-shih-koh oo-chee-dah), the daughter of Takashi Uchida, about whom you read in Chapter 2, reported, "My diploma, rolled in a cardboard container, [was] handed to me in my horse stall [at Tanforan Assembly Center in California] by the Tanforan mailman."

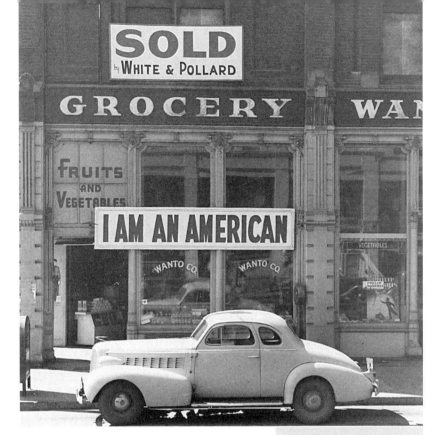

Many Japanese Americans were forced to sell their business in the short time before evacuation. The Wanto family received a fraction of their store's value when they were forced to sell.

For some Nisei, the war and the evacuation shattered the dream of getting an education and a good job. Iwato Itoi (ee-waht-oh ee-toi) was studying to be an aviation mechanic at a technical school. When the war came, he and other students of Japanese ancestry were told to leave. Looking back on this experience years later, he said:

> When they kicked us out, I mean the whole thing went black, and it just wiped me out. . . . I'm still bitter about that, you know. My whole life is just ruined. . . . That was my dream school, you know. To become a master aviation mechanic.

When the war was over, Itoi became a gardener. Whenever a plane flew overhead, he thought of the work he could have been doing if he had been allowed to finish his education.

While some students like Itoi were bitter, others struggled to accept what was happening. A student newspaper in California published a letter from a young Nisei:

> True, we are being uprooted from the lives that we have always lived, but if the security of the nation rests upon our leaving, then we will gladly do our part. We have come through a period of hysteria, but we cannot blame the American public for the vituperations [abuse] of a small minority of self-seeking politicians and special interest groups. We cannot condemn democracy because a few have misused the mechanism of democracy to gain their own ends.

What Will I Leave Behind? As the day of evacuation drew near, families frantically tried to dispose of household goods. Some found neighbors who would let them store their beds and dressers and family treasures in unused garage or basement space. Evacuees sold what they could not store. Refrigerators worth $100 were sold for $10 or $15. Furniture sets went for much less than their value. One woman became very angry when a dealer offered her $15 for a $200 setting of china. Instead of selling, she smashed the dishes on the ground.

But not all of people's worries were over money or material goods. Many Japanese Americans felt sad at leaving the place where they had grown up and lived for many years. One Nisei remembered, "Staring at the ceiling in bed at night, I wondered who would take care of my cherry tree and my house after we moved out."

TAKING ANOTHER LOOK

1. What special problems did the evacuation create for businesspeople and farmers?
2. Why were evacuees often unable to get a fair price for their household goods?
3. *CRITICAL THINKING* How did the disruptions in evacuees' lives compare to the disruptions that German Americans experienced during the war years?

2 FIRST STOP: ASSEMBLY CENTER

What was the evacuation like for Japanese Americans?

The government's plan was to evacuate the Japanese families first to one of 16 **assembly centers** that had been hastily set up at racetracks and fairgrounds in California, Washington, and Arizona. The evacuees would stay in these centers from the spring of 1942 until the fall, while workers built the more permanent camps elsewhere where people of Japanese descent were to be interned.

On the morning of departure, after a night of fitful sleep, people awoke to empty homes that echoed eerily when they spoke. Many had slept their last night on the floor. They had sold their beds or placed them in storage. After a hurried breakfast, people grabbed their carefully labeled bags and headed for an assembly site—a church, a community center, or just a street corner.

Buses and Armed Guards. In her book *Nisei Daughter*, Monica Itoi Sone (soh-nay) described how the evacuation went for her:

Their car overloaded, this Japanese American family in Los Angeles sadly waits to leave for an assembly center.

[Buses came.] The bus doors opened and from each, a soldier with rifle in hand stepped out and stood stiffly at attention by the door. The murmuring died. It was the first time I had seen a rifle at such close range and I felt uncomfortable. This rifle was presumably to quell riots, but contrarily, I felt riotous emotion mounting in my breast.

Soldiers and Civilians Buses and trains carried the evacuees to the assembly centers. The U.S. Army was in charge of the initial evacuation. It also ran the assembly centers. However, the federal government had set up a special civilian agency to run the camps where the evacuees would eventually end up. The civilian agency was called the War Relocation Authority (**WRA**). Its first director was Milton Eisenhower. He was the brother of the general who would become famous during the war and would later be President Dwight D. Eisenhower.

The U.S. government called these places "assembly centers" and "relocation centers," but they were really more like concentration camps. The centers were places where women, men, and children were interned without a trial or any evidence of guilt. As an internee, Yoshico Uchida explained:

"Assembly center" and "relocation center," terms employed to designate the concentration camps in which we were incarcerated [imprisoned], were also a part of the new terminology developed by the United States government and the Army to misrepresent the true nature of their acts.

While these WRA centers were not death camps as the Nazi concentration camps were, some people in them did commit suicide and a few were actually killed by guards.

Going Quietly One reason the evacuation went smoothly was that Japanese Americans by and large cooperated. No one wanted to be singled out as a complainer. The Japanese had a saying: *Deru kugi utareru* (deh-roo

A former horse stall at a California race track was "home" for Japanese Americans as they waited to be sent to the WRA internment centers.

koo-gee oo-tah-reh-roo)—"The nail that sticks up the farthest takes the most pounding." When they were told they had to leave their homes and be herded off to camps, people went quietly. For most, it would have been unthinkable to defy the government.

The leading organization of Japanese Americans, the Japanese American Citizens League (JACL), also concluded that resistance to evacuation would only increase hostility against Japanese Americans. Said JACL leader Saburo Kido (sah-buh-roh kee-doh):

> When we leave our homes, let us leave with a smiling face and courageous mien [appearance]. Let us look upon ourselves as the pioneers of a new era looking forward to the greatest adventure of our time.

The JACL had been organized in the 1920s to lobby for better treatment for Japanese Americans. It accepted only Nisei American citizens as members. Over the years, the

JACL had struggled to end the ban on naturalization of Asians. It had also fought against other discriminatory measures, such as California's Alien Land Law. In the weeks leading up to evacuation, JACL members had worked long and hard. They supplied food and services to families in need of assistance.

However, not all Japanese Americans agreed with the JACL's approach. During the years of internment, arguments often broke out between critics and supporters of the group. Critics called the JACL leaders "stooges" of the U.S. government and accused them of betraying the interests of Issei and Nisei alike. You will read more about those arguments in later chapters.

TAKING ANOTHER LOOK

1. What was the difference between assembly centers and WRA camps?
2. Why did the Japanese American Citizens League advise people to cooperate with the federal government?
3. *CRITICAL THINKING* If you had been ordered to evacuate, would you have cooperated or resisted? Explain.

3 LONELY EXILE

Where did the evacuees go and what did they find when they arrived?

The first things people noticed when they arrived at the assembly centers were the barbed wire and the bayonets of the soldiers who stood guard. Then they noticed the dust and mud. Since the assembly centers had been adapted from other uses, they provided only the simplest of quarters—four walls, a roof, a bed. Little more.

Making Do Tar-papered barracks had been hastily nailed together to provide these accommodations. But some families had even simpler facilities. For Yoshiko Uchida, at the Tanforan center in California, "home" was now to be a converted horse stall:

We pushed open the narrow door and looked uneasily into the vacant darkness. The stall was about ten by twenty feet and empty except for three folded Army cots lying on the floor. Dust, dirt, and wood shavings covered the linoleum that had been laid over manure-covered boards, the smell of horses hung in the air.

The evacuees immediately noticed the lack of privacy. Walls between the "apartments" were so thin that people could hear even the whispers of their next-door neighbors. Often, families of three, four, and more shared a single room.

For some teenagers and younger children, camp life promised adventure, but for the older Issei it was a severe trial. Yoshiko Uchida describes watching her mother as they waited in line for supper the first night:

> Shivering in the cold, we
> pressed close together
> trying to shield Mama
> from the wind. As we
> stood in what seemed a

In which states were most assembly centers located? Why? In which states were the relocation (internment) camps? Why do you think people called them by the term relocation camps?

INTERNMENT CENTERS FOR JAPANESE AMERICANS, 1942-1946

EVACUATION AREAS
▲ Assembly Centers
■ WRA Camps
Areas from which people of Japanese descent were evacuated, 1942

45

breadline for the destitute [the very poor], I felt degraded (disgraced), humiliated, and overwhelmed with a longing for home. And I saw the unutterable sadness on my mother's face.

Adapting to Camp Life   The evacuees gradually adapted to life in the assembly camps. They looked forward to the days when non-Japanese friends would visit, perhaps bringing a small gift like an apple or a bag of nuts. Each camp resident received **scrip**, or camp money, with which to buy toothpaste and other items. Some of the evacuees were religious leaders, and they organized Buddhist and Christian services.

The evacuees had to endure many small attacks on their self-respect. Twice each day, someone would come around to count heads, to make sure no one had escaped. Occasionally men would come to search for forbidden goods such as guns. Evacuees had to hand over their Japanese-language books—even Bibles. Buddhist leaders had to rewrite their services in English.

Before long, school classes were organized to allow young people to continue their education. Adults could attend classes in English or in such subjects as flower arranging and first aid.

On to WRA Camps   After three months or so, word came that the camps where the evacuees were to be interned were ready. The evacuees boarded trains. They traveled for hours, sometimes for days.

Two of the ten WRA internment camps—Tule Lake and Manzanar (MAN-zah-nahr)—were in California. Six others were scattered across other states in the West: two in Arizona, one each in Utah, Idaho, Wyoming, and Colorado. The two WRA camps that were farthest east were in Arkansas. (See the map on page 45.)

A summer sun blazed down on the plains when a trainload of evacuees reached Idaho's Minidoka internment camps. One of the passengers wrote:

The train stopped at the end of the tracks which was right in the midst of sagebrushes, and dust.

VERSE FROM THE PAST

Some evacuees turned to poetry to express their feelings about life in the assembly centers. The two poems below were written at the Tanforan center in California. Their author, who goes by the pen name Yukari (yoo-kah-ree), is the mother of writer Yoshiko Uchida.

Plate in hand,
I stand in line,
Losing my resolve
To hide my tears.

Four months have
passed,
And at last I learn
To call this horse stall
My family's home.

It was a desolate-looking place and down in the bottom of my heart, I started feeling homesick for the green trees [and] . . . the Puget Sound [of Washington]. . . . I could feel the struggle inside of me to keep the tears from coming up.

Near the Minidoka camp headquarters stood a billboard bearing a stinging reminder of why the evacuees were there. The billboard proclaimed: "Remember Pearl Harbor."

TAKING ANOTHER LOOK

1. **a.** What sorts of living accommodations did evacuees have at the assembly centers? **b.** How did they "make do"?

2. In which states were WRA camps located?

3. *CRITICAL THINKING* What aspects of life in the assembly centers made the evacuees feel like prisoners?

CHAPTER 3: CLOSE UP

1 Saying Goodbye

- The evacuation of West Coast Japanese Americans began in the spring of 1942.
- Interruptions to the lives of business owners, farmers, and students caused special problems.
- Because each person could take only two bags, families had to store or sell most of their belongings, often suffering tremendous financial losses.

2 First Stop: Assembly Center

- The evacuees went first to army-run assembly centers to await construction of more permanent WRA camps.
- Japanese tradition taught respect for authority, so most evacuees went along quietly. The Japanese American Citizens League advised dignified cooperation.

3 Lonely Exile

- The assembly centers offered simple accommodations with little privacy and many small attacks on evacuees' self-respect.
- Camp life included classes for children and adults and both Buddhist and Christian religious services.
- The evacuees remained at assembly centers for about three months, then were transferred to camps run by the WRA.

WHO, WHAT, WHERE

1. **Where** were people of Japanese descent ordered to evacuate from?
2. **What** were evacuees allowed to take with them?
3. **Where** did people gather for evacuation?
4. **What** was the Japanese American Citizens League?
5. **What** part of the federal government was in charge of the evacuation to assembly centers?
6. **What** agency of the government operated the WRA camps?
7. **Where** were the 16 assembly centers located?

8. **Where** were the ten WRA camps located?

1. How did the evacuation cause Japanese Americans to suffer financial losses?
2. Why did the evacuees have to stay in assembly centers before moving to the WRA camps?
3. What aspects of the evacuation made Japanese Americans feel like criminals or prisoners?
4. Why did most Japanese Americans cooperate with authorities and accept evacuation quietly?
5. What did people do to occupy their time in the assembly centers?

1. What was the connection between the armed soldier whom Monica Itoi Sone saw and the "riotous emotion" she felt?
2. What was the connection between the army's role in the evacuation and the War Relocation Authority's role?

1. Imagine that your own family is about to be evacuated and confined to a camp in wartime. Using the Japanese American experience in World War II as a model, draw up a written plan describing the preparations your family should make and the items each family member would take along in two suitcases or duffel bags.
2. Imagine that you are living at the time of the Japanese American evacuation. Whatever your own ancestry, do you accept the evacuation or challenge it? Describe what you would do and why.
3. Write a memo to the leaders of the Japanese American Citizens League setting forth arguments both for and against cooperating with the evacuation.
4. Write a brief skit in which members of your class will act out one of the events described in this chapter. Use your imagination to create a realistic dialogue.

LIFE IN THE WRA CAMPS

THINKING ABOUT THE CHAPTER

How did evacuees occupy their time during the months and years they spent in the WRA camps?

Miyo Senzaki (mee-yoh sehn-zah-kee) does not smile when she remembers being in the WRA internment camp at Rohwer, Arkansas. She recalls:

> I had this really sad feeling. . . . You couldn't run anywhere. It was scary because there was no end to it. You could run and run and run but where are you to go? It was just nothing but water and then there were rattlesnakes. We felt like prisoners.

SECTIONS

1 Behind Barbed Wire

2 Negative Public Attitudes

3 Cooperation or Resistance?

Rohwer and Jerome in Arkansas were the only camps built on swampland. The other camps, in the Western states, were mainly in deserts. No one had lived on the sites before the war, and no one would live there after the war. Most of the sites could be described as empty and lifeless. Temperatures soared as high as 135°F (57°C) in summer and plunged as low as -35°F (-37°C) in winter.

▲
Nov. 3, 1942
Last evacuees reach WRA centers from assembly camps.

▲
July 31, 1943
Tule Lake Relocation Center becomes the camp for "disloyal" evacuees.

▲
Feb. 3, 1943
The War Relocation Authority begins to administer the loyalty questionnaire to all evacuees 17 years of age or older.

▲
Jan. 28, 1943
Army restores right of Japanese Americans to volunteer for military service.

▲
July 18, 1944
63 Heart Mountain draft resisters are sentenced to three-year prison terms.

▲
July 15, 1943
WRA announces plan to segregate "disloyal" evacuees.

▲
Jan. 20, 1944
Authorities resume drafting of Japanese Americans.

1 BEHIND BARBED WIRE

How was life in the WRA camps more difficult than life elsewhere in wartime United States?

For the evacuees, life seemed to stand still during the months or years they spent in the camps. They found plenty to do—keeping warm, getting fed, struggling to make it through the day—but little was interesting or stimulating. The government officials who ran the camps viewed them as "little cities" that were not much different from other U.S. communities. But the evacuees had only to look at the barbed-wire fences and guard towers. They knew the truth—they were prisoners, jailed without trial solely because of their ethnic background.

"Cookie Cutter" Camps Looking down on the WRA camps from an airplane, one might have thought that some giant, using a cookie cutter, had stamped out nearly identical communities in ten different places. The camps followed one basic pattern—that of an army camp.

The typical WRA internment center was built to hold 10,000 people. The evacuees lived several families to a **barrack**, a building that serves as living quarters for soldiers. The barracks were arranged in blocks of two rows of six barracks each. Each block had its own bathing and toilet facilities. The average center contained 36 blocks of barracks, but the number varied. For instance, the camp at Topaz, Utah, had 42 such blocks of barracks. Scattered through the camp were mess halls, where meals were served, and buildings for recreation, medical care, and schools. Around the entire camp were barbed-wire fences, with towers where armed men stood guard.

More than anything else, the evacuees objected to the barbed wire and the guard towers. In a petition sent to the War Relocation Authority director, a group of evacuees at Heart Mountain, Wyoming, called the barbed wire "an insult to any free human being." It meant, they said, that their camp was a "concentration camp" and that they were "prisoners of war." The letter brought no changes. The barbed wire remained.

WRA "Apartments" At first, most of the barracks had a single layer of boards for walls, with tar paper covering the roofs. Gaps between the boards let in howling winds and gritty dust. Weeds grew up through cracks in the floors. Small coal and wood stoves supplied heat, so fires were a constant threat. Before the first winter was over, crews put up wallboards and ceilings. That helped a bit to hold in heat and fend off cold.

Families lived in what the WRA called apartments. These were actually rooms without partitions. The smallest apartments measured 20 feet by 8 feet while the largest were 20 feet by 24 feet. An apartment of 480 square feet was assigned to families of six. Only large families had more than one room.

Schools in the Camps The camp directors tried to get schools started as soon as possible. They wanted to give young people something to do and keep them from falling behind in their studies. In many cases, the first classes met in unheated rooms without textbooks. Supplies were so scarce at Tule Lake, California, that a typing class had to

make its own "typewriters." An evacuee explained: "We drew circles on a sheet of paper, lettered the circles, and practiced by pressing our fingers over the circles."

The teachers were of uneven quality. Some were fellow evacuees with college educations, others were credentialed white teachers, and a few even had PhDs. Some were sympathetic to the students and proved to be dedicated, effective teachers. Others were just putting in time until something better came along. Probably the most effective teachers were those who expected their students to maintain high standards in spite of the barren school environment.

In time, the schoolrooms were heated, and students acquired supplies. Nearby public schools sent old textbooks. Religious organizations donated storybooks and encyclopedias. Sports equipment arrived, and teams from the camps competed against teams from nearby schools. The Nisci students formed after-school clubs and planned school proms, bravely pretending that they were ordinary students in ordinary U.S. communities. But at times—such as when reciting the Pledge of Allegiance—contrary thoughts surfaced. Jack Matsuoka (maht-soo-oh-kah), for example, thought that the Pledge "somehow sounded hollow. Even the teacher's voice trailed off to a murmur at the part about liberty and justice for all."

Helping to Supply the Nation Many of the evacuees were farmers or gardeners, and they put their skills to good use. All the camps set up farms that supplied the camp kitchens with pork and sometimes poultry and beef. One camp had its own dairy. The farms grew most of a camp's vegetables, and some even supplied nearby cities. Evacuees in some camps went to work on neighboring farms.

With U.S. industries struggling to meet the demand for war materials, the camps pitched in. Three camps set up factories to make camouflage nets to conceal U.S. troops from the enemy. Some ran sawmills.

Low Rates of Pay Despite these contributions, there were still newspaper charges that the government was "coddling" (pampering) the evacuees. Thus the War Relocation Authority paid them very low wages. It made sure that no evacuee would earn more than the lowest-ranking U.S. soldier. At the start of the war, an army private earned $21 a month, so evacuee wages were kept below that level. The pay was $19 a month (about 11 cents an hour) for teachers and other skilled workers. Less-skilled workers received $16 a month, unskilled laborers $12.

The low pay angered many of the evacuees. They thought it was unfair that a non-Japanese camp librarian, for example, received $167 a month, while the staff of evacuees received $16 each. From time to time, groups of evacuees would strike for higher pay. But the pay scale never changed—even when the government doubled the pay of soldiers.

Making the Best of It Realizing that they might be interned a long time, evacuees set to work to make the camps more livable. They bought curtains from mail-order catalogs for barrack windows. They gathered rocks to create rock gardens. When spring came, they planted "victory gardens" to supply extra vegetables. They also planted flowers and fruit trees.

The evacuees organized activities to make use of their spare time. For the young, there was baseball, football, and

Ten World War II WRA Camps

	Date Opened	Date Closed	Maximum Population
Gila River, Arizona	7-20-42	11-10-45	13,348
Granada, Colorado	8-24-42	10-15-45	7,318
Heart Mountain, Wyoming	8-12-42	11-10-45	10,767
Jerome, Arkansas	10-6-42	6-30-44	8,497
Manzanar, California	6-1-42	11-21-45	10,046
Minidoka, Idaho	8-10-42	10-28-45	9,397
Poston, Arizona	5-8-42	11-28-45	17,814
Rohwer, Arkansas	9-18-42	11-30-45	8,475
Topaz, Utah	9-11-42	10-31-45	8,130
Tule Lake, California	5-27-42	3-20-46	18,789

Name the three largest and three smallest of the WRA camps.

Japanese sumo wrestling. Young musicians formed groups to play for weekend dances. Girls and boys joined Scout troops. Adults attended classes in English, doll-making, first aid, Japanese calligraphy (the art of writing characters), and many other subjects. In addition, Buddhists and Christians held religious services.

However, most evacuees grumbled about the restrictions of camp life and longed to be back home. But a few found the camps a pleasant escape from their ordinary cares. Some even admitted that they enjoyed camp life. It was a sad commentary on the prejudice and discrimination that Japanese Americans had faced before December 7, 1941.

TAKING ANOTHER LOOK

1. In what ways was life in the WRA camps more difficult than life outside them?
2. What challenges did the camp schools face?
3. *CRITICAL THINKING* Why did some evacuees in the camps feel that they were "prisoners of war"?

2 NEGATIVE PUBLIC ATTITUDE

What picture did the public have of life in the WRA camps?

Some newspapers set out to convince their readers that the evacuees had much better lives than the average U.S. citizen. As a result, many people believed that while their own sons and daughters were fighting and dying in a distant war, Japanese Americans were "on vacation" in comfortable camps.

Hostile Reporting Leading the attack on the "soft" treatment of the evacuees were newspapers like the Denver *Post*. In 1943, the Post reported finding "carloads" of the "finest oranges" and other "luxury fruits and rare vegetables" in storerooms at Heart Mountain, Wyoming. A *Post* headline read:

FOOD IS HOARDED FOR JAPS IN U.S.
WHILE AMERICANS IN NIPPON [Japan]
ARE TORTURED

Congress quickly launched an investigation. Officials of the War Relocation Authority responded that the storerooms contained extra food because the evacuees' food ration had been cut. Because of wartime shortages, the government had imposed **rationing**. That is, it allowed people to receive only limited amounts of certain items like gasoline, sugar, and other foods. But some people refused to listen. One member of Congress claimed that evacuees at Heart Mountain were "using tractors and gas for amusement and races." Moreover, he said, they "are demanding—and getting—prime beef and five gallons of whiskey apiece."

This hostile publicity further inflamed opinion against Japanese Americans. To counter such publicity, Heart Mountain held an open house in August 1943 so that reporters could see for themselves how evacuees lived. No one saw luxury.

Sympathy from Some Despite the anti-Japanese mood, a portion of the public sympathized with the evacuees. Religious groups such as the Quakers (or Friends)

WE DON'T WANT ANY JAPS BACK HERE--EVER!

Despite the hardships the internees faced, people continued to be hostile. This man from Kent Washington is reacting to the news that Japanese Americans may return to Kent when the war is over.

worked to get the evacuees released. The American Friends Service Committee and other religious groups appealed for 50,000 Christmas gifts to be sent to the camps.

Many of the evacuees were deeply grateful for these efforts. Remarked author Yoshiko Uchida, "In many cases correspondences and friendships developed that lasted long after the war ended, and we were touched by the compassion [sympathy] and concern some Americans felt for us."

Flawed "Self-Government" Officials in charge of the camps set up "governments" elected by the evacuees to run them. The authorities allowed only U.S. citizens to hold office in the camp councils. That meant that Nisei could be leaders but their parents, the Issei, could not. Both groups were allowed to vote, however.

TAKING ANOTHER LOOK

1. How did the general public feel about the treatment of Japanese Americans in the WRA camps?
2. How did some people show sympathy for the evacuees?
3. *CRITICAL THINKING* Why do you think so many U.S. citizens believed unfounded charges about conditions in the internment camps?

3 COOPERATION OR RESISTANCE?

What happened when the authorities asked evacuees to affirm their loyalty to the United States?

The scene: the entrance to a laundry room at a WRA camp. One evacuee is going in, another is coming out. As they meet, their lips curl in disgust. "Inu [ee-noo]," one growls. "Fascist," snarls the other. Inu means "dog" in Japanese. In the camps, some evacuees called anyone who cooperated with U.S. authorities a "dog" or "traitor." Evacuees who used the term were angry at the U.S. government. Some were also sympathetic to Japan.

Fascist is a word that describes the undemocratic form of government of Japan's allies, Germany and Italy, before and during the war. The term also means a supporter of such governments. Like the fascists, Japan's leaders glorified military might and ruled with an iron fist. Such policies horrified evacuees who considered themselves loyal U.S. citizens. They looked down on evacuees who sympathized with Japan and sometimes called them fascists.

Loyalty Questionnaires In January 1943, the U.S. government reversed its wartime policy of barring Japanese Americans from the armed forces. The government planned to form a segregated, all-Nisei unit to fight in the war in Europe. But it wanted to make sure that any Nisei recruited were genuinely loyal to the United States. It decided to ask all adult male U.S. citizens in the camps to fill out a questionnaire that included the following questions:

• Are you willing to serve in the armed forces of the United States, wherever ordered?

• Will you swear unqualified allegiance to the United States of America . . . and forswear [give up] any form of allegiance or obedience to the Japanese Emperor, or any other foreign government, power, or organization?

The War Relocation Authority distributed a similar questionnaire to female and Issei adults in the camps. The WRA questionnaire was inappropriately labeled Application

HONORING EVACUEES

The site of the Manzanar Relocation Camp in eastern California is now a national historical landmark. It serves to honor Japanese Americans and remind future generations of the wrongs done to evacuees during World War II.

Year after year, former evacuees and sympathizers make a pilgrimage to the lonely site. From 1942 to 1945, Manzanar was the largest "city" between Los Angeles and Reno, Nevada. But when the war ended, almost all its buildings were torn down. Today, in a setting of sand and sagebrush, visitors see a small cemetery where evacuees who died in the camp are buried. They also see two stone guardhouses, built by an evacuee.

Twenty busloads of people attended the dedication of the landmark in 1992, 50 years after the evacuation. They gathered in small groups to talk about their own experiences. They heard speeches vowing that such things must never happen again.

Organizers of that year's pilgrimage dedicated it to Ralph Lazo [LAH-soh], a Mexican American. Lazo was 17 when his Japanese American friends were sent to Manzanar. He did not want to remain free when his friends were not free. Lazo moved to the camp along with his friends and stayed there for two years before being drafted into the army.

for Leave Clearance. But it did not matter if people wanted to apply. Everyone had to fill it out.

How to Answer? The evacuees agonized over how to answer the questions. For women and elderly Issei, some questions made no sense. They could not serve in the military. Many Issei were afraid that if they answered "yes" to both questions they would become people without a country. Although they were not eligible for U.S. citizenship, a "yes" answer to the questions could mean losing their Japanese citizenship.

Some Nisei men readily answered "yes." They were eager to serve in the U.S. Army. They thought, What better way do we have to show our patriotism and regain our full rights as U.S. citizens? The JACL supported that position. One camp newspaper printed in an editorial: "There is too much at stake to brood over the injustices of the past."

But some Nisei men who saw themselves as loyal Americans answered "no" to the questions. They insisted that they should first regain their full rights by being freed from the camps. Then, as free citizens, they could join the army.

Disputes over the questionnaires caused great anguish in many of the camps. Said Hanayo Inouye:

> My husband and I thought that since our children were born in the United States, we would sign "yes." Then some people accused us by saying, "What kind of fools are you to say 'yes' to a country that's treating us like this?" Oh, they were angry at us. . . . Many of our long-time friendships were broken as a result.

In the end, the vast majority of evacuees answered "yes" to both questions. The War Relocation Authority labeled as "disloyal" anyone who had answered "no." Such people were sent to the camp at Tule Lake, California. So were people who had asked for repatriation.

Restoration of the Draft Early in 1944, the army reclassified Nisei men and made them subject to selective service—the military draft. To JACL leaders, the new policy was a sign that Japanese Americans were being restored the full rights of citizens. Said league leader Mike Masaoka (mah-sah-oh-kah):

> When the war is won, and we attempt to find our way back into normal society, one question which we cannot avoid will be, "Say, Buddy, what did you do in the war?" If we cannot answer that we, with them, fought for the victory which is ours, our chance for success and acceptance will be small. We need Selective Service.

But others saw it differently. A small but militant draft resistance sprang up in camps like Manzanar and Heart Mountain. Leaders of the movement urged Nisei men to test the draft law by insisting on full citizenship rights be-

fore responding to a draft call. At Heart Mountain, 54 of the first 315 men ordered to report for physical examinations did not show up.

Under the watchful eyes of guards Japanese Americans attempted to go on day to day until they were free to leave.

In wartime, resisting the draft was a serious offense. The government quickly cracked down. In a mass trial in Cheyenne, Wyoming, a judge convicted 63 Nisei draft resisters and sentenced them to three years in prison.

Authorities also charged leaders of the resistance movement with conspiring to urge others to break the draft laws. A jury convicted seven of those leaders. However, an appeals court reversed these convictions. The number of Nisei draft resisters was relatively small—315 in all. By the time the war ended, some 26,000 Nisei had volunteered for the armed forces or had been drafted.

TAKING ANOTHER LOOK

1. How did the evacuees react to the loyalty questionnaires?

2. What changes in U.S. policy in 1943 and 1944 opened up new opportunities for male Nisei in the camps?

3. *CRITICAL THINKING* One evacuee wrote after the war was over, "I believe it required uncommon courage [for men of draft age] to make either decision [to answer "yes" or "no" on the questionnaires] under intolerable circumstances." Do you agree or disagree with this statement? Explain.

CHAPTER 4: CLOSE UP

1 Behind Barbed Wire

- The ten WRA camps housed about 10,000 people. Evacuees lived in barracks, ate in mess halls, and shared central bathroom facilities.
- Guards and barbed-wire fences made the evacuees feel that they were in concentration camps.
- Evacuees held important jobs in the camps, but their wages were kept very low.
- Camp activities included schools for children, classes for adults, and a variety of recreational activities.

2 Negative Public Attitude

- Hostile publicity convinced much of the public that U.S. authorities were pampering the evacuees.
- Some outsiders tried to befriend the people in the camps.
- The camps set up "self-governments" with limited powers. Issei could not hold elective positions.

3 Cooperation or Resistance?

- The authorities had evacuees fill out questionnaires that asked about their loyalty. Resistance and confusion resulted.
- A change in U.S. policy in 1943 allowed Japanese Americans to volunteer for military service. In 1944, Japanese Americans became subject to the draft.
- Many evacuees quickly took advantage of the chance to serve their country. However, some resisted, demanding a restoration of their full rights as citizens first.

WHO, WHAT, WHERE

1. **What** is Nippon?
2. **What** does *incarcerated* mean?
3. **What** are barracks?
4. **What** was the War Relocation Authority's response to the petition to remove the barbed wire?
5. **What** did some typing students use for typewriters?
6. **What** "sounded hollow" about the Pledge of Allegiance?

7. **What** did evacuees do to fill the time in the camps?

8. **What** is rationing?

9. **Who** was called *inu*? Why?

10. **What** is a fascist?

1. Describe the physical layout of the camps and the way the evacuees spent their time.

2. **a.** What aspects of the camps did the evacuees most dislike? Why? **b.** What did some evacuees like about the camps? Why?

3. How did workers within the camps contribute to the U.S. war effort?

4. **a.** What was the purpose of the loyalty questionnaires? **b.** How did evacuees respond to them?

5. Why did some Japanese Americans applaud the restoration of the draft for Nisei men?

1. What was the connection between a soldier's pay and the pay earned by evacuees in the WRA camps?

2. What was the connection between answering "no" on the questionnaires and the Tule Lake camp?

1. Write a short story about a chance encounter between an off-duty guard and an evacuee at one of the camps.

2. Imagine that you are a non-Japanese person employed in a WRA camp. Write a letter to a friend back home describing your feelings about your work.

3. Imagine that you are a Nisei who is editor of your camp newspaper. Write an editorial suggesting how evacuees should respond to the resumption of the draft for Japanese American men.

GETTING OUT

How could Japanese Americans
win release from the WRA
camps in order to pursue
more normal lives?

Behind the barbed-wire fences of their camps, Japanese Americans dreamed of the outside world and freedom. Young people missed being able to go to town for an ice-cream soda. Adults missed their old homes. How long would they have to remain behind barbed wire, people wondered. When would they regain their freedom?

In the WRA camp at Poston, Arizona, Henry Tanda found an answer. He learned that the WRA authorities would let "loyal" Japanese Americans leave the camp if they could find jobs away from the West Coast military zones. Tanda discovered that a farmer in Montana wanted workers. Tanda told his wife, "We can go to Montana if you'll cook for eight fellows."

She quickly agreed. They received permission to leave, and boarded a train for Montana with their two small daughters and eight young men from the camp. A few miles from the Canadian border, they began a new life as free U.S. citizens once more.

SECTIONS

1 Going to Work,
Going to College

2 Going to War

3 Going Home

▲
June, 1942
100th Battalion leaves
Hawaii for training in
Wisconsin.

▲
Feb 3, 1943
Army forms all
Nisei 442nd Infantry
Regiment Combat
Team.

▲
July 15, 1946
President Truman
presents Presidential
Distinguished Unit
Citation to 442nd
Infantry regiment in
Washington. D.C..

▲
June, 1944
442nd Infantry Regiment
begins fighting in Italy;
joins 100th Battalion
north of Rome.

▲
Sep., 1943
100th Battalion joins in
Allied invasion of Italy
at Salerno,
south of Rome.

▲ Dec. 17, 1944
Oct., 1944 Army withdraws its evacuation
442nd Infantry Regiment orders, ending the legal basis for
liberates Bruyeres; rescues "lost keeping Japanese Americans in
battalion" of Texans. camps.

1941 ▲   1942 ▲   1943 ▲   1944 ▲   1945 ▲   1946 ▲   1947 ▲

Between 1942 and 1945, as the war raged across Europe and the Pacific, thousands of Japanese Americans regained their freedom. Even as they were arriving at the WRA camps in 1942, the WRA was making plans to let some of them leave. It set up two programs. One was for work that could be done during certain seasons, such as harvesting crops. The other was for permanent jobs, like the one the Tandas found. WRA policies also allowed some Japanese Americans to leave the camps to attend college or to join the armed forces. However, most older Japanese Americans remained in the camps until 1945.

1 GOING TO WORK, GOING TO COLLEGE

What opportunities for work and education were open to people in the WRA camps?

During the spring and summer of 1942, farmers in many Western states looked at their ripening fields and wondered how they would manage the harvest. Many farmers and farmhands had gone to war. Who would take their places? The farmers' thoughts turned to the Japanese Americans being held in camps. Growers asked federal officials to allow Japanese Americans to help bring in the harvest. The officials agreed. Between 1942 and 1944, thousands of Japanese Americans were allowed to leave the camp to do seasonal farm work.

Although the work on the farms was hard, many welcomed the chance at outside labor. For one thing, pay was higher than in the WRA camps. For another, returning to "the outside world" was exciting. One worker wrote:

> We went out to the farm in an old truck and we
> felt wonderful to have our freedom once more. It
> was such a good sensation to be moving along
> those dirt roads away from camp. As we traveled
> along further, I filled my eyes with the sight of
> green lawns, individual homes, paved streets,
> and actual water fountains.

Mixed Reception The workers from the WRA camps did not always feel welcome on the outside. People in the Western states had mixed feelings about the Japanese Americans. They made this clear in letters to public officials. One citizen wrote the governor of Utah, "I've heard club women talk of boycotting farmers all over the state who hire Japs." There were fears expressed that the Japanese Americans would poison the fruit they picked.

Elected officials responded to people's fears. They stated that they did not want Japanese Americans to remain in their states when the war was over. Many states passed laws aimed to that effect. Wyoming, for example, granted certificates to Japanese American teachers that limited them to teaching only in the WRA camps, not in regular schools.

However, many other Westerners appreciated the work the Japanese Americans did. A Utah labor official declared, "If it had not been for Japanese labor, much of the [1942] beet crop of Utah and Idaho . . . would have been plowed up."

Off to College The WRA allowed students who passed a loyalty test to leave the camps for colleges and universities. However, the students were not permitted to attend schools on the West Coast. But many colleges in the Midwest, East and South welcomed Nisei students.

At first, strict rules applied. One rule barred Japanese Americans from colleges that were within 25 miles (40 kilometers) of "strategic sites" such as railroad stations. Another rule prevented Japanese Americans who had visited Japan from leaving the camps for school. Later, some of the restrictions were eased. By the end of 1942, 250 students had been released for college study. Eventually, the figure reached 4,300.

To gain release from WRA camps, Japanese American internees volunteered for farm labor. These Japanese American internees were released so they could pick peaches on farms in the U.S. Midwest.

Long-Term Work Leave The WRA tried to find permanent jobs away from the West Coast for as many Japanese Americans as possible. There were a number of reasons why the WRA was so interested in finding jobs outside the camps. It wanted to speed the return of Japanese Americans to normal life. At the same time, it wanted to reduce the cost of running the camps. During 1943, the WRA slashed the number of jobs in the camps. Without jobs, it figured, more people would apply for jobs outside the camps.

Because of the wartime labor shortage, many companies recruited people from the camps. A frozen-food firm in southern New Jersey hired 2,600 Japanese Americans. Railroads needed workers. Hotels needed help. Farmers needed hired hands. Japanese Americans gladly took such jobs.

1. Why did Western farmers need seasonal workers from the WRA camps?

2. What restrictions were placed on college students leaving the camps?

3. *CRITICAL THINKING* It is 1943. You are interned in a WRA camp. How would you respond to the complaint that Japanese Americans are being released from the WRA camps?

2 GOING TO WAR

What role did Japanese Americans play in World War II for the United States?

The time was October 1944. All day long the people of Bruyères (broi-YAIR) in northeastern France huddled in their cellars as bombs exploded around them. Then suddenly there was silence. One man cautiously poked his head out and looked around. The German troops who had occupied Bruyères for the past four years were gone. But who were those uniformed men who had taken their place? The soldiers appeared to be Japanese. Were they from Japan, Germany's ally? As the man stood there puzzled, one of the soldiers smiled and pointed to his chest. "Hawaiian," he said. "Okay, okay."

The men were U.S. soldiers. They belonged to a special unit of the U.S. Army, the Japanese-American 442nd Infantry Regiment. After the war, the grateful people of Bruyères renamed one of the main streets the "rue de la 442e" ("Street of the 442nd").

On the Battlefronts Japanese Americans had to put up a fight to be allowed to serve in the war. First, they had to convince U.S. authorities that they were loyal U. S. citizens. Then they had to struggle for combat roles in the armed forces. However, once the military command accepted Japanese Americans, they proved to be outstanding soldiers. Many won medals for bravery in battle.

Some 27,000 Japanese Americans fought in Europe.

Students who passed a loyalty test were also allowed to continue their studies. These students attending Park College in Parkville, Missouri take part in a flag raising ceremony.

Another 6,000 served in the Pacific, mainly in the Military Intelligence Service. Most of those who served were men. Some Japanese American women served in the Women's Army Corps and as nurses.

Most of the Japanese Americans who fought in Europe were part of the 442nd Infantry Regiment. Others served in Hawaii's 100th Battalion. Almost all of the soldiers in the 442nd and the 100th were Japanese Americans. Their commanding officers, however, were white.

Ben Kuroki, War Hero One of the first Japanese Americans to become a hero of World War II was a Nebraska farm boy named Ben Kuroki. Despite the discrimination against Japanese Americans, Kuroki managed to join the Army Air Force soon after Pearl Harbor. At first, officers wanted to keep him working at low-level jobs. But Kuroki persuaded them to let him become a gunner on bombers. He flew bombing missions over North Africa and Europe.

On one mission, Kuroki's plane and many others flew deep into enemy territory to strike at Romanian oil refineries. Of the 56 planes that set off on the 13-hour flight, only Kuroki's and one other returned. All the rest were shot down.

Kuroki won the Distinguished Flying Cross and became a nationally known hero. Headlines hailed him when he visited the WRA camp at Heart Mountain, Wyoming, in April 1944. He appealed to young Nisei to "fight for our country, America." This helped to weaken the draft resistance movement at the camp.

The 100th Battalion While Joe Takata was in high school, he was a star baseball player for a team in the Hawaiian League. When the war came, he traded his baseball uniform for that of a sergeant in the 100th Battalion. When the battalion joined in the Allied invasion of Italy in September 1943, Takata was killed. He was the first member of the 100th to die in battle and one of 48 Japanese Americans to win the Distinguished Service Cross.

The 100th Battalion was part of the Hawaii National Guard. Most of its members were **draftees**, men who had been chosen to serve, rather than volunteers. As its motto, the battalion adopted the slogan: "Remember Pearl Harbor."

The 442nd Regiment Unlike the 100th Battalion, many of the men in the 442nd were volunteers who had spent time in WRA camps. They were eager to prove their loyalty to flag and country. In the words of Tom Kawaguchi, "I joined because I always felt strongly about patriotism; I felt that this was my country. I didn't know any other country."

One of the 442nd's most celebrated deeds took place during the liberation of France in 1944. The regiment rescued a unit of Texans called "the lost battalion." The Texans had been cut off from their regiment 9 miles (14.4 kilometers) behind enemy lines, near Bruyères. Rescuing them seemed to be a hopeless job. But the 442nd battered away at the German lines and eventually managed to reach the Texans. But it lost three men for every one it rescued. "[O]ut of my company of 230 men, I was one of the 23 men to walk out," recalled Shig Doi of the 442nd.

Rifles at the ready members of the 442nd Infantry Regiment move across a bridge on the way to fighting in Italy.

Interpreting for the Army
Meanwhile, other Japanese Americans were helping to win the war in the Pacific. Many Nisei had learned Japanese at home. In the army, they put their knowledge of Japanese to work intercepting messages and questioning enemy captives.

During a 1943 battle off the island of New Guinea, Allied forces captured a mass of Japanese documents. Working day and night for six days, a team of Japanese Americans translated them. The documents listed the names of 300,000 enemy soldiers, telling where each one had served in the past and where he was serving now. That information made U.S. officials realize how thinly the Japanese forces were stretched. The Japanese American translators had helped reveal that Japan was not so strong as it seemed to be.

Honors and Achievements Germany surrendered in May 1945 and Japan in August 1945. Yet even before then, Japanese Americans had won new respect from other Americans. Headlines about "Nisei war heroes" deeply impressed the public. As a result, many Americans who had once been hostile to Japanese Americans changed their minds.

Things also improved for Japanese Americans thanks to the GI Bill of Rights of 1944. Under this bill, the government provided money for veterans to attend college. It also lent veterans money to start businesses and buy homes. U.S. Senator Daniel Inouye (see page 18), who served in the 442nd, declared that the GI Bill helped Japanese Americans to get better educations and build better lives. "It made possible the dramatic postwar rise of the Japanese Americans," he said.

In July 1946, the soldiers of the 442nd Infantry Regiment paraded proudly through the nation's capital. In a ceremony on the White House lawn, President Harry S Truman awarded a presidential medal on the unit for its accomplishments. Said Truman:

> You fought not only the enemy, you fought prejudice, and you have won. Keep up that fight, and continue to win—-to make this great Republic stand for just what the Constitution says it stands for: "the welfare of all of the people, all of the time."

Thankful for a safe return from war, members of the 442nd and their wives celebrate the docking of their troopship at San Francisco in 1945.

1. **a.** What Japanese American military unit was made up mainly of Hawaiians? **b.** What military unit contained many men from the WRA camps?
2. How did Japanese Americans benefit from the GI Bill?
3. *CRITICAL THINKING* In World War II, U.S. Army units were segregated. There were all-white, all-African American, and all-Asian American units. Do you think the public would have been as positive about Japanese American soldiers if the soldiers had been integrated into military units with other Americans? Why or why not?

3 GOING HOME

What did Japanese Americans find when they were at last able to return home?

Rifleman Wilson Makabe of the 442nd Infantry Division lay in a military hospital in Italy. While his shattered body was slowly healing, he dreamed of going home to his family's fruit farm in Loomis, California. His family had been forced to leave the farm in 1942. Now, with the end of the war in sight, his parents were as eager as their son to return home.

Makabe was put on a plane for home. When the plane landed in New York City, he telephoned his brother. It was two days before Christmas in 1944. His brother told him that hours after the announcement that Japanese Americans could return home, someone had set fire to the family house in Loomis.

> When he told me that . . . oh, you can't describe the feeling. I remember the pain and the hurt, the suffering in the hospitals in Italy. That was nothing compared to this. I cried for the first time. . . . You wonder if it was worth going through all that.

Six days earlier, on December 17, 1944, the army had announced that Japanese Americans could return to their homes as of midnight on January 2, 1945. The news an-

KRISTI YAMAGUCHI, STAR FIGURE SKATER

Kristi Yamaguchi, world champion figure skater, does not dwell on her family's past, but she can't really forget it. Her mother, Carole Doi Yamaguchi, was born in a WRA camp in Colorado in 1945. At the time, her father, Kristi's grandfather, was fighting in Europe with the 100th Battalion. Kristi's father, Jim Yamaguchi, also lived behind barbed wire. He was four years old when his family was taken off their California farm to a WRA camp in Arizona.

"We've told our children about the camps," Jim Yamaguchi said. "They can't really understand the experience, though." The camps had been closed for more than 25 years by the time Kristi Yamaguchi was born. Growing up in Fremont, California, she gave little thought to her family background. "I always thought of myself as just an American," she said.

When Kristi Yamaguchi won the gold medal for figure skating at the 1992 Winter Olympics in France, she became the first Japanese American world-class skater. The residents of Fremont—Japanese and non-Japanese alike—turned out for a big parade to welcome Kristi home after she won the gold medal. It was Kristi Yamaguchi Day in Fremont, and wartime memories seemed far away.

gered many West Coast residents, who had hoped that Japanese Americans would not be allowed to return even after the war. Some people took out their anger by attacking Japanese Americans. Others destroyed their property.

However, there were some residents who were pleased that their neighbors would be coming home. They helped to set up places where the returning Japanese Americans could stay while they looked for permanent living quarters.

Home Again For some Japanese Americans, homecoming was a celebration. Kane Kozono, for example, received a warm welcome from her neighbors in West Sacramento. "One of our neighbors visited us right away with a lot of vegetables from the family garden," she said. "Everybody welcomed us back."

Masao Hirata had more serious problems. Hirata recalled:

> When we returned to California, we didn't have a place to live. One of my friends leased me this small house. . . . My farm had not been touched for five years, and I didn't even have any tools to cut down the tall weeds on the land. But I had to work to support my family, so I borrowed old tools and worked on my farm. Every Japanese person had to start again from the beginning.

Rather than return to the West Coast areas from which they had been removed, many Japanese Americans settled in the Midwest, East, and South. The wartime evacuation thus served to spread Japanese Americans across the nation.

Return to Japan Of the 120,000 Japanese Americans who were interned, some 4,700 decided to return to Japan after the war. There they had to "start again from the beginning." They faced extreme shortages of food and housing. Kazue Yamane said, "We subsisted on sweet potatoes for two or three weeks and then on leaves of sweet potatoes for two or three weeks."

Some of those who chose **repatriation**, return to their country of birth, were not happy in Japan. Kazue Yamane, for example, sent two of her children back to the United States. "The war devastated Japan, and we were not accepted in Japan either, first of all because we were different" she said. About 1,100 Japanese American adults had given up their U.S. citizenship. Many applied to get it back. Eventually, the United States returned citizenship to 685 of those people.

TAKING ANOTHER LOOK

1. Why were not all Japanese Americans released from the WRA camps when the war ended?

2. What problems did returning Japanese Americans face?

3. *CRITICAL THINKING* Why do you think many of the people who chose return to Japan had trouble fitting into Japanese society?

CHAPTER 5: CLOSE UP

1 Going to Work, Going to College

- After loyalty checks, the WRA let some Japanese Americans leave the camps for work or college.
- Many Japanese Americans took seasonal jobs such as fighting fires and harvesting crops in Western states.
- Because of the wartime labor shortage, many companies recruited Japanese American workers from the camps for permanent jobs away from the West Coast.

2 Going to War

- About 33,000 Japanese American men and women served in the armed forces during World War II. Most of them were on the European front.
- The main Japanese American units in Europe were the 100th Battalion (from Hawaii) and the 442nd Infantry Regiment. The 442nd was mainly recruited from WRA camps. Both units suffered heavy casualties.
- After the war, the GI Bill helped Japanese American veterans to buy homes, start businesses, and go to college.

3 Going Home

- The army lifted its ban on Japanese Americans in West Coast areas at the end of 1944. The WRA camps closed down gradually, over the next 14 months.
- Violence greeted some Japanese Americans, but others received a warm welcome from their neighbors.
- With little help from the government, Japanese Americans had to rebuild their lives.

WHO, WHAT, WHERE

1. **What** crops did Japanese Americans help to harvest?
2. **Where** did students from the WRA camps go to college?
3. **Where** is Bruyères? Why was the town grateful to Japanese Americans?
4. **What** was the 442nd Infantry Regimental Combat Team?
5. **What** was the 100th Battalion?
6. **Where** did Japanese Americans serve in the Military Intelligence Service?

7. **Who** was Ben Kuroki?

8. **What** was the GI Bill of Rights?

UNDERSTANDING THE CHAPTER

1. Why were many Japanese Americans eager to get jobs outside the WRA camps? What reason did the WRA have for encouraging Japanese Americans to take permanent outside jobs?

2. What requirement did Japanese Americans have to meet before they were allowed to leave the WRA camps for work or college?

3. How did all Japanese Americans benefit from the military service of Japanese American draftees and volunteers during World War II?

4. What problems did Japanese Americans face when the government released them from the WRA camps?

MAKING CONNECTIONS

1. What was the connection between the 100th Battalion and the 442nd Infantry Regiment?

2. What was the connection between the GI Bill of Rights and the postwar economic advancement of Japanese Americans?

WRITING ABOUT HISTORY

1. Imagine that you are a Japanese American in a WRA camp. Write a description of the steps you will have to take to get a permanent job away from the camp.

2. Suppose that you are a newspaper editor in a farming area where Japanese Americans are helping to harvest the crops. Write an editorial urging the community to welcome the workers.

3. Imagine that you are a Nisei and have volunteered for military service in World War II. Your parents oppose the idea. Write a letter explaining to them the reasons for your action.

RIGHTING THE WRONG

THINKING ABOUT THE CHAPTER

How have people in the United States changed their view about the wartime internment of Japanese Americans?

The internment of Japanese Americans was "one of the most sweeping and complete deprivations [denials] of constitutional rights in the history of this nation." Those were the words of Supreme Court Justice Frank Murphy. He wrote them in 1944 when an appeal against the U.S. government's actions reached the Court. But Murphy was only one Justice among nine. Most of his fellow Justices saw things differently. They approved the internment.

By the 1980s, however, the mood of the nation had changed. Courts took a fresh look at the wartime actions, and so did Congress. In 1988, Congress voted to apologize. The apology was part of a bill authorizing the payment of $20,000 to each survivor of the wartime camps. In signing the bill, President Ronald Reagan declared, "No payment can make up for those lost years. What's most important in this bill has less to do with property than with honor. For here, we admit a wrong."

That apology did not come easily. Japanese Americans struggled for years to get it. They went to court, lobbied Congress, and carried their case to the public. By the time they won their point, only half of the 120,000 Japanese Americans who had been interned were still living.

Timeline

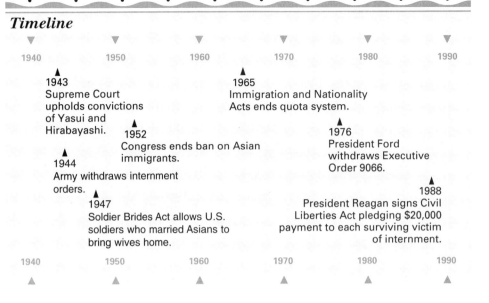

1940 — 1950 — 1960 — 1970 — 1980 — 1990

1943
Supreme Court upholds convictions of Yasui and Hirabayashi.

1952
Congress ends ban on Asian immigrants.

1944
Army withdraws internment orders.

1947
Soldier Brides Act allows U.S. soldiers who married Asians to bring wives home.

1965
Immigration and Nationality Acts ends quota system.

1976
President Ford withdraws Executive Order 9066.

1988
President Reagan signs Civil Liberties Act pledging $20,000 payment to each surviving victim of internment.

1940 — 1950 — 1960 — 1970 — 1980 — 1990

1 CHALLENGES IN COURT

How did U.S. courts respond to challenges against the internment during the war years? What happened when the courts took a second look many years later?

For Minoru Yasui (mee-NAWR-oo ya-soo-ee), the nation's apology came too late. Yasui had died in 1986. That was 44 years after the government threw him in jail for violating the nighttime curfew placed on Japanese Americans living along the West Coast. Yasui was one of a number of Japanese American citizens who refused to accept the government's wartime actions.

Challenging the Curfew When World War II started, Minoru Yasui was a young Nisei lawyer. In 1939, he had become the first Japanese American to graduate from the University of Oregon Law School. Because no major law firm in Oregon would hire a Japanese American, Yasui went east. He took a job in a Japanese government office in Chicago.

As soon as he learned of the attack on Pearl Harbor,

Yasui quit his job and joined the U.S. Army. As a former cadet in the Reserve Officer Training Corps, he expected to serve as an officer. But when he reported for duty, officials told him to go home. They said no U.S. soldier would take orders from a Japanese American. Hurt and angry, Yasui moved to Portland, Oregon. He offered his legal services to members of the Japanese community who wanted to protect their homes and property.

After President Roosevelt issued Executive Order 9066, the military authorities ordered people of Japanese ancestry to observe a curfew. Minoru Yasui believed the curfew was a clear violation of constitutional rights. He informed the FBI that he planned to challenge it. One night he left his home after the curfew had begun.

Yasui walked up to a police officer and showed him his birth certificate and a copy of the curfew order. The officer refused to arrest Yasui. So he walked to a police station and showed the officers the same documents. This time he was arrested. A judge fined him $5,000 and sentenced him to a year in jail. What's more, he said Yasui had lost his U.S. citizenship by working for the Japanese government.

In jail, Yasui was kept in a windowless cell by himself. For months his jailers did not allow him to shave or get a haircut. Yasui waited for the Supreme Court to rule on his appeal. In June 1943 the ruling came. The Court unanimously found that the curfew was legal. It approved the fine and jail term. However, the Court ruled that Yasui was still a U.S. citizen.

Released from jail after nine months, Yasui spent most of the war years in the WRA camp in Minidoka, Idaho. When the government allowed Nisei to join the armed forces, Yasui toured several camps to urge young men to volunteer.

Gordon Hirabayashi (hee-rah-bah-yah-shee), a college senior in Seattle, also turned himself in for violating the curfew. He faced a second charge as well: refusing to obey the internment order. In 1943 the Supreme Court upheld Hirabayashi's conviction on the curfew count. It refused to consider his challenge to the internment.

Challenging the Internment The Supreme Court dealt with the internment of Japanese Americans the following year. It did so in the case of Fred Korematsu (kawr-

Forty years after their clash with the government Fred Korematsu, Minoru Yasui, and Gordon Hirabayshi, left to right, meet at a 1983 San Francisco press conference.

eh-maht-soo). Korematsu was a welder in the Oakland area of California. He was planning to move to the Midwest, outside the military zone. So when the internment order came, he ignored it—and was arrested.

In the case of *Korematsu v. United States*, the Supreme Court again sided with the federal government. By a vote of six-to-three, the Justices accepted the government's argument that military need justified extreme measures. For the majority, Justice Hugo Black wrote that "pressing public need may sometimes justify restrictions" on a minority.

Justice Robert H. Jackson wrote a strong **dissent**—an opinion disagreeing with the majority's view. He described the Court's ruling as "a loaded weapon ready for the hand of any authority that can bring forward a plausible [more or less reasonable] claim of an urgent need." Jackson warned that the decision might come back to haunt the nation in some future emergency. Jackson said the Court's decision might be twisted into support for even more sweeping measures against a minority group.

Winning Release The only Japanese American to win a major case against the government during the war was Mitsuye Endo (mit-soo-yee ehn-doh). She did not resist internment orders. Instead, once she arrived at a WRA camp she applied for work leave. The WRA found her to be a loyal citizen and thus eligible for work leave. However, it did not accept her request to return to California. It kept her in the camp, so she sued.

In December 1944, the Supreme Court ruled unanimously that the WRA had no authority to hold citizens indefinitely in internment camps once they had been found to be loyal. Endo must be freed. While that was an important finding, it was limited. The Court made clear that it was not declaring internment illegal.

A Second Look After the war, researchers began to look into the wartime records of federal government departments. They found that the military commander for the West Coast had relied on stereotypes rather than facts in ordering the internment. The FBI had reported finding no evidence that Japanese Americans were a threat to the nation's wartime security. But FBI reports had been kept secret from the courts.

In the early 1980s, Yasui, Hirabayashi, and Korematsu all took their cases back to court. All three had their convictions reversed. In the Korematsu case, Ninth District Court Judge Marilyn Hall Patel sharply criticized the government. She said that "the government deliberately omitted [left out] information in papers before the court."

The 1980s decisions cleared the records of the three Japanese Americans. They also reminded the nation that governments can make mistakes, especially under the stresses of wartime. As Judge Hall warned, "[I]n times of distress the shield of military necessity and national security must not be used to protect governmental actions from close scrutiny."

TAKING ANOTHER LOOK

1. What were the issues in the Yasui, Hirabayashi, and Korematsu cases?

2. How did the Endo case differ from the others?

3. *CRITICAL THINKING* Why is it more difficult to protect civil rights during wartime than in peacetime?

2 MAKING AMENDS

After the war, how did Japanese Americans seek to persuade the U.S. public that they had suffered a great wrong?

As you have read, farmers had lost their land. Storékeepers had had to sell their businesses at below-market prices. Homeowners had lost their homes because they could not keep up monthly home payments. Thousands of Japanese Americans had suffered major economic losses because of their forced internment. The Federal Reserve Bank of San Francisco estimated the total losses at $400 million.

Efforts to recover those losses began as soon as the war ended. The Japanese American Citizens League (JACL) took its appeals to Congress and to the public. However, very few Japanese Americans got back what they had lost. Decades passed before the U.S. public admitted that the internment had been a mistake.

Ending Executive Order 9066 in 1976, President Gerald Ford was in the company of distinguished Americans including, behind the President, Daniel Inouye and Patsy Mink.

Lowering Immigration Barriers Japanese American groups like the JACL fought to end the discrimination against Asians in U.S. immigration laws. One early victory came when Congress passed the **Soldier Brides Act of 1947**. That act allowed U.S. soldiers who had married Asians to bring their spouses to the United States after the war. Without the new act, the brides would have been barred because of the ban on Asians in the 1924 immigration law (page 12). Another new law in 1948 allowed Asians who had served in the U.S. armed forces in either world war to become U.S. citizens.

Far more significant were new laws that opened the doors of the United States to more Japanese immigrants. In 1952, Congress ended the exclusion of Asian immigrants. But it kept the quota system, giving Japan a quota of just 185 immigrants a year.

The **Immigration and Nationality Act of 1965** opened the door more widely to immigration from Asia by putting an end to the quota system. The law placed all immigrants from outside the Western Hemisphere into one big "pool." It gave Asians equality with Europeans. Among those invited to witness the signing of the 1965 law was Mike Masaoka. As a leader of the JACL, he had worked hard to pass the new law.

Seeking Compensation Restrictions on Japanese ownership of property fell away during the 1950s and 1960s. California's Supreme Court struck down that state's alien land law (page 11) in 1952. Four years later, California voters agreed to repeal the law. Over the next ten years, other states abolished their alien land laws too. The JACL lobbied Congress for a law to pay back Japanese Americans for the losses they had suffered in the internment. In 1948, Congress passed the **Evacuation Claims Act**. More than 23,000 Japanese Americans filed claims. The largest was for more than $1 million; the smallest, for a child's tricycle. However, the government challenged most of the claims. Furthermore, the average payment was about 10 percent of what Japanese Americans were seeking. All told, internees collected about $38 million.

Many Japanese Americans believed that the government payments were highly inadequate. In the early 1970s,

Three elderly Japanese Americans who had been interned almost half a century before, received $20,000 checks and an apology from Attorney General Dick Thornburgh in 1988.

some members of the JACL began to push for further action. They said the government should do more to **redress,** or correct, the harm it had done.

A First Apology The first fruits of this movement came in 1976. In that year, President Gerald Ford canceled Executive Order 9066, which had been the legal basis for the internment (see page 29). Ford called the wartime internment a "mistake." He added:

> We now know what we should have known then. Not only was that evacuation wrong, but Japanese Americans were and are loyal Americans.

Japanese American leaders applauded Ford's statement as a first step. But some leaders urged the government to go further. They proposed a payment to all internees—a payment that would help to compensate them for the economic losses they had suffered during their years of internment. To establish the need for such compensation, the JACL persuaded Congress to set up a special commission to evaluate the wartime policies.

PATSY MINK: SPEAKING OUT

Patsy Takemoto (tah-keh-moh-toh) was a girl of 14 when West Coast Japanese Americans were confined in internment camps. Because she and her family were residents of Hawaii, however, they remained free. After the war, Takemoto rose to a position of prominence in Hawaiian politics. Under her married name, Patsy Mink, she won national attention by speaking out on women's rights issues.

As a U.S. Representative in the early 1970s, Mink promoted a measure that became Title IX of the Education Amendment Act of 1972. Title IX barred sex discrimination in schools and colleges that accepted federal funds. Law schools and medical schools had to admit more women. School sports programs had to be open equally to males and females.

Mink began her political career in the mid-1950s when Hawaii was still a U.S. territory. She was an active member of a group of young Democrats in the territorial legislature who pushed for stronger action to fight poverty.

Mink first entered Congress in 1965 and served in the House for 12 years. Her stay in Washington broke off when she tried for a Senate seat in 1976. She lost to Spark Matsunaga in the Democratic primary. After a break of more than 10 years, Mink won reelection to the U.S. House of Representatives in 1990.

"A Grave Injustice" The Commission on the Wartime Relocation and Internment of Civilians took testimony around the country. In 1983, it issued its report. Sharply criticizing the wartime policy, the commission said:

> Executive Order 9066 was not justified by military need. The broad historical causes which shaped decisions were race prejudice, war hysteria, and a failure of political leadership. . . . A grave injustice was done to American citizens of Japanese ancestry who, without individual review or any evidence against them, were excluded, removed and detained by the United States .

The commission recommended a $20,000 payment to each surviving internee to compensate him or her for the injustice of the internment.

Paying Compensation Laws to carry out the commission's recommendation won strong backing in Congress. Key supporters included Senators Daniel Inouye (in-oh-way) and Spark Matsunaga (maht-soo-nah-gah) of Hawaii and Representatives Norman Mineta and Bob Matsui (maht-soo-ee) of California—all Japanese Americans. Congress soon passed the compensation bill, which became the **Civil Liberties Act of 1988.**

As the bill neared final passage, a handshake between Representative Mineta and Senator Alan Simpson of Wyoming brought back memories of their first meeting in a WRA internment camp years before. Mineta was detained at the Heart Mountain camp with his family. Simpson lived in nearby Cody, Wyoming. They met when Simpson came with his Boy Scout group to visit Japanese American Scouts in the camp. "Somehow we got paired and sort of hit it off," Mineta recalled. They kept up their acquaintance after the war. Simpson was one of many cosponsors of the bill to compensate the internees.

President Ronald Reagan signed the bill on August 10, 1988. A few weeks later, Canada's government also agreed to make payments to people of Japanese ancestry whom it had detained during the war. Supporters of the payments wanted to do more than pay Japanese Americans back for their losses. They wanted to remind all people in the United States of a tragic time in their history—so that it would not happen again.

TAKING ANOTHER LOOK

1. What changes in immigration laws in the 1950s and 1960s put Asians and Europeans on equal footing?
2. What was the key finding of the Commission on the Wartime Relocation and Internment of Civilians?
3. *CRITICAL THINKING* In your opinion, what is the most important lesson that the United States can draw from the wartime internment of Japanese Americans?

CHAPTER 6: CLOSE UP

1 Challenges in Court

- During World War II, the Supreme Court upheld the internment of people of Japanese ancestry. The Court said that military necessity justified the actions.
- Only one Japanese American won a wartime challenge to the regulations. It was a limited victory that came one day after the army had agreed to let the internees return home.
- During the 1980s, courts learned that the federal government had concealed important facts in the wartime cases. Judges reversed the convictions of three Japanese Americans.
- Nonetheless, the Supreme Court's wartime decisions upholding internment remained the "law of the land."

2 Making Amends

- The United States lifted its ban on Asian immigration in 1952. In 1965 the government ended the quota system, putting Asian immigrants on equal footing with European immigrants.
- California and other states ended restrictions on land ownership by noncitizens in the 1950s and 1960s.
- A national commission concluded in 1983 that the wartime treatment of Japanese Americans was not based on military necessity and had caused "a grave injustice."
- In 1988, Congress voted to apologize and to pay $20,000 to each of the 60,000 surviving internees.

WHO, WHAT, WHERE

1. **Who** was Minoru Yasui?
2. **Who** was Gordon Hirabayashi?
3. **Who** was Fred Korematsu?
4. **What** is a dissent (in a court decision)?
5. **Who** was Mitsuye Endo?
6. **Where** did Endo want to go for her work leave?
7. **What** was the Soldier Brides Act of 1947?
8. **What** was the Immigration and Nationality Act of 1965?

9. **Who** was Mike Masaoka?

10. **What** was the Evacuation Claims Act of 1948?

UNDERSTANDING THE CHAPTER

1. On what grounds did the Supreme Court uphold the internment of Japanese Americans?

2. What findings in the 1980s raised questions about the government's conduct in the wartime court cases?

3. What did Justice Robert H. Jackson mean by calling the Supreme Court decision in the Korematsu case "a loaded weapon"?

4. How did Japanese Americans finally manage to get the federal government to apologize for its wartime actions?

MAKING CONNECTIONS

1. What was the connection between the Commission on the Wartime Relocation and Internment of Civilians and Congress's decision to pay compensation to internees?

2. What was the connection between Norman Mineta and Alan Simpson?

WRITING ABOUT HISTORY

1. Suppose you are a friend of Minoru Yasui and you are discussing his plan to challenge the curfew on Japanese Americans. He asks what you would do in his place. What do you respond—and why?

2. Suppose you are the clerk of a Supreme Court Justice at the time of the Korematsu case. The Justice asks you for your opinion. Write a memo giving reasons for either joining the majority or joining Justices Murphy and Jackson in dissent.

3. Imagine that you are a former internee who has been called to testify before the Commission on the Wartime Relocation and Internment of Civilians. You have two minutes to tell your story. What will you say?

4. Suppose you were one of the internees who spent the war in a W.R.A. internment camp. Recently, a grandchild asked: "What was it like?" Write your response in a letter.

Time Chart

The Time Chart below shows events that were taking place around the world during the years studied in this book.

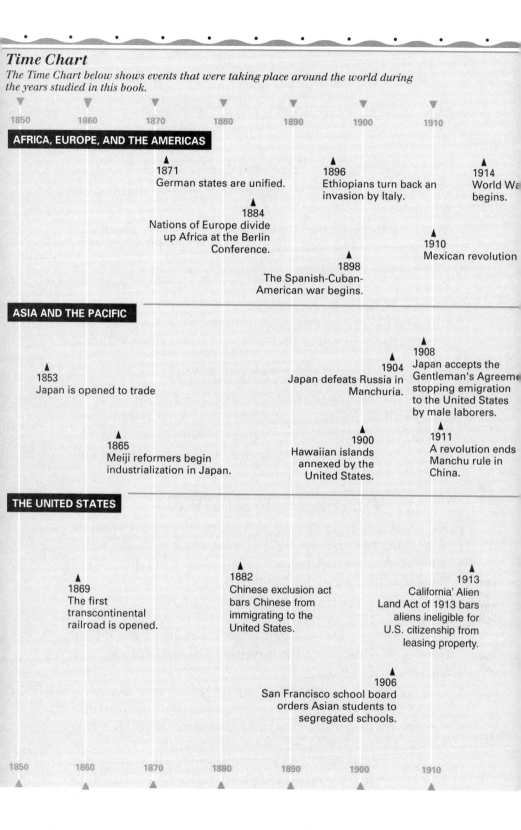

1850   1860   1870   1880   1890   1900   1910

AFRICA, EUROPE, AND THE AMERICAS

1871
German states are unified.

1896
Ethiopians turn back an invasion by Italy.

1914
World War begins.

1884
Nations of Europe divide up Africa at the Berlin Conference.

1910
Mexican revolution

1898
The Spanish-Cuban-American war begins.

ASIA AND THE PACIFIC

1853
Japan is opened to trade

1904
Japan defeats Russia in Manchuria.

1908
Japan accepts the Gentleman's Agreement stopping emigration to the United States by male laborers.

1865
Meiji reformers begin industrialization in Japan.

1900
Hawaiian islands annexed by the United States.

1911
A revolution ends Manchu rule in China.

THE UNITED STATES

1869
The first transcontinental railroad is opened.

1882
Chinese exclusion act bars Chinese from immigrating to the United States.

1913
California' Alien Land Act of 1913 bars aliens ineligible for U.S. citizenship from leasing property.

1906
San Francisco school board orders Asian students to segregated schools.

1850   1860   1870   1880   1890   1900   1910

▲
1922
The Ottoman Empire
is abolished.

▲
1939
World War Two
breaks out in Europe.

▲
1917
Russian Revolution
brings Communists
to power.

▲
1945
Germany
surrenders ending
war in Europe.

▲
1937
Japan extends its
control over China.

▲
1930
Japan invades China.

▲
1937
United States stops all
shipments of iron, steel
and oil to Japan.

▲
1941
Japan bombs
Pearl Harbor,
Hawaii.

▲
1945
Japan agrees to
unconditional surrender.

▲   ▲
1942   1943
President Roosevelt 100th Battalion joins in Allied
orders mass evacuation invasion of Italy at Salerno,
of all people of south of Rome.
Japanese ancestry.

▲
1988
President
Reagan signs
Civil Liberties
Act pledging
$20,000
payment to
each surviving
victim of
internment.

▲
1924
ration act of 1924 ends the
ntleman's Agreement and
s all immigration by aliens
ineligible for citizenship.

▲
1965
Immigration and
Nationality
Act ends quota system.

▲   ▲
1942   1943
xecutive Order 9066 authorizes military areas from War relocation authority begins to
which any or all persons might be evacuated. administer the loyalty questionnaire
to all evacuees 17 years or older.

▲
1944
442nd Infantry regiment liberates Bruyeres; rescues
"lost battalion" of Texans.

▲
1952
Congress ends
ban on Asian
immigrants.

▲
1976
President Ford
withdraws Executive
Order 9066.

GLOSSARY

The glossary defines important terms used in the book. The page on which a term first appears is given in parentheses at the end of the definition.

Alien Land Law of 1913 Forbade the purchase of farm land by aliens ineligible for citizenship **(p. 11)**

annex take control of a territory **(p. 7)**

boycott refuse to purchase or use certain goods or services **(p. 23)**

Chinese Exclusion Act law that banned all immigration to the United States by Chinese **(p. 8)**

Civil Liberties Act of 1988 Law providing compensation for all living Japanese American survivors of internment **(p. 87)**

contract laborers workers who agree to work on a job for a certain period of time **(p. 7)**

curfew a time after which people cannot leave their houses **(p. 31)**

draftees people who were selected to serve in the armed forces by the government **(p. 70)**

embargo a government ban on goods from another country **(p. 23)**

enemy aliens citizens of enemy nations during wartime **(p. 24)**

evacuate be forced to leave an area **(p. 36)**

Evacuation Claims Act law passed in 1948 to repay the losses of Japanese Americans who had suffered in the internment **(p. 84)**

evacuees the people to be evacuated **(p. 37)**

Immigration Act of 1924 ended immigration for all aliens ineligible for citizenship **(p. 12)**

imperialism the conquest of foreign lands **(p. 20)**

interned confined in prison camps **(p. 26)**

Inu Japanese for traitor. Literally means "dog." **(p. 58)**

Issei first generation Japanese who moved to the United States **(p. 10)**

Japanese American Citizen League (JACL) group organized in 1920s to lobby for better treatment for Japanese Americans **(p. 43)**

kimono wide-sleeved Japanese robe **(p. 4)**

labor contractor person who supplies work crews to farmers **(p. 13)**

League of Nations an association of nations organized to promote international peace and cooperation **(p. 22)**

martial law rule by the military. Soldiers patrol the streets and administer the laws **(p. 30)**

naturalized citizens aliens who gain citizenship **(p. 10)**

picture brides Japanese women who were known to their husbands-to-be in the United States only by photographs **(p. 5)**

rationing regulation in which people receive limited amounts of certain items such as gasoline and sugar **(p. 56)**

repatriation return to the country of one's birth **(p. 75)**

Soldier Bride Act of 1947 law that allowed U.S soldiers to bring their Asians spouses to the United States **(p. 84)**

Varsity Victory Volunteers (VVV) Japanese Americans who formed a special labor battalion to help the U.S. Army Corps of Engineers **(p. 33)**

INDEX

SOURCES

Sources for quotations are given by page number (in parentheses) and in the order in which the quotations appear on each page. **CHAPTER 1** (9) Riichi Satow, quoted in Eileen Sunada Sarasohn, *The Issei: Portrait of a Pioneer: An Oral History* (Palo Alto, California: Pacific Books, 1983), pp. 24-26. (13) Sarasohn, pp. 116-121. (15) Yoshiko Uchida, *Desert Exile: The Uprooting of a Japanese American Family* (University of Washington Press, 1982), p. 40. **CHAPTER 2** (18-19) Dan Inouye, recalled in Daniel K. Inouye with Lawrence Elliott, *Journey to Washington* (Englewood Cliffs, New Jersey: Prentice-Hall, Inc., 1967), pp. 54-55. (20) John Toland, *The Rising Sun: The Decline and Fall of the Japanese Empire, 1936-1945, Vol. 1* (New York: Random House, 1970), p. 236. (26) Robert S. Yasui, *The Yasui Family of Hood River, Oregon* (Williamsport, Pennsylvania: Robert S. Yasui, 1987), pp. 13-14. (28) Henry McLemore, quoted in *San Francisco Examiner*, January 20, 1942, cited in Roger Daniels, Sandra C. Taylor, and Harry H. L. Kitano, *Japanese Americans: From Relocation to Redress* (University of Utah Press, 1986), pp. 80, 86. (29) Daniels, p. 76. (29-30) Chester Rowell, quoted in Audrie Girdner and Anne Loftis, *The Great Betrayal: The Evacuation of the Japanese-Americans During World War II* (Toronto: Macmillan, 1969), p. 31-32. (32) Lieutenant General Delos C. Emmons, quoted in Girdner and Loftis, pp. 20-21. (32) Wilson and Hosokawa, *East to America* (New York: Morrow, 1980), p. 155. **CHAPTER 3** (36) Emi Somekawa, quoted in John Tateishi, *And Justice for All: An Oral History of the Japanese American Detention Camps* (New York: Random House, 1984), pp. 146-151. (38) Florence M. Hongo and Miyo Burton, *Japanese American Journey: The Story of a People* (San Mateo, California: Japanese American Curriculum Project, Inc., 1985), p. 118. (38) Yoshiko Uchida, quoted in Uchida, p. 89. (39) Iwato Itoi, quoted in Tateishi, pp. 141-145. (40) Takae Washizu, quoted in Sarasohn, p. 166. (42) Monica Itoi Sone, quoted in Sone, *Nisei Daughter* (Boston: Little, Brown, 1953), pp. 169-179. (43) Tateishi, p. 37. (44) Saburo Kido, quoted in Girdner and Loftis, p. 127. (45-46) Uchida, p. 70. (48) Daniels, Taylor, and Kitano, p. 106. **CHAPTER 4** (50) Miyo Senzaki, quoted in Tateishi, p. 103. (52) Douglas W. Nelson, *Heart Mountain: The History of an American Concentration Camp* (University of Wisconsin Department of History, 1976), p. 84. (53) Commission on Wartime Relocation and Internment of Civilians, *Personal Justice Denied* (Washington, D.C.: U.S. Government Printing Office, December 1982), p. 171. (53) Jack Matsuoka, quoted in Jack Matsuoka, *Camp II, Block 211: Daily Life in an Internment Camp* (Tokyo: Japan Publications, 1974), p. 151. (56) Nelson, pp. 59-61, 66. (58) Nelson, p. 99. (60) *Heart Mountain Sentinel*, February 27, 1943, quoted in Nelson, pp. 107-108. (60) Hanayo Inouye, quoted in Sarasohn, p. 210. (60) Mike Masaoka, quoted in Mike Masaoka with Bill Hosokawa, *They Called Me Moses Masaoka: An American Saga* (New York: Morrow and Co., 1987), pp. 120-21. **CHAPTER 5** (64) Henry Tanda, quoted in Girdner and Loftis, p. 341. (66) Dorothy Swaine Thomas, *The Salvage* (University of California Press, 1952), p. 253. (66) Daniels, Taylor, and Kitano, p. 95. (66) Girdner and Loftis, p. 339. (68) Masayo Umezawa Duus, *Unlikely Liberators: The Men of the 100th and 442nd* (Honolulu: University of Hawaii Press, 1987), p. 6. (70) Tom Kawaguchi, quoted in Tateishi, p. 180. (72) Daniel Inouye, quoted in Duus, p. 235. (72) Harry S Truman, quoted in Tomi Kaizawa Knaefler, *Our House Divided: Seven Japanese American Families in World War II* (Honolulu: University of Hawaii Press, 1991), p. 25. (73) Wilson Makabe, quoted in Tateishi, p. 255. (74) Jim Yamaguchi, quoted in Ann Killion, "Soul on Ice: Yamaguchi Family Endured Internment," San Jose *Mercury News*, March 13, 1989. (74) Kristi Yamaguchi, quoted in Jody Meacham, "A Position of Honor: Yamaguchi's Success Is a Triumph for Ethnic Pride," San Jose *Mercury News*, March 26, 1992. (74-75) Kane Kozono, quoted in Sarasohn, p. 255. 75) Kazue Yamane, quoted in Tateishi, p. 137. **CHAPTER 6** (78) Jacobus tenBroek, Edward N. Barnhart, and Floyd W. Matson, *Prejudice, War, and the Constitution: Causes and Consequences of the Evacuation of the Japanese Americans in World War II* (University of California Press, 1954), p. 2. (78) Ronald Reagan, quoted in San Jose *Mercury News* (Stock Final), August 10, 1988 (Mercury Library via America Online). (81) Justice Hugo Black, quoted in *Korematsu v. U.S., 323 us 214* (1944), 216-220, quoted in Daniels, Taylor, and Kitano, p. 182. (81) Justice Robert H. Jackson, quoted in Girdner and Loftis, p. 377. (82) Judge Marilyn Hall Patel, quoted in Daniels, Taylor, Kitano, pp. 201-202. (85) Gerald Ford, quoted in Wilson and Hosokawa, p. 297. (86) Daniels, Taylor, and Kitano, p. 5. (87) Norman Mineta, quoted in New York Times News Service, "Reparations Forged by Pair from Opposite Sides of Barbed Wire," San Jose (California) *Mercury News*, April 26, 1988.